Nationalisms

Nationalisms

*The Nation-State and Nationalism in
the Twentieth Century*

MONTSERRAT GUIBERNAU

Polity Press

First published in 1996 by Polity Press
in association with Blackwell Publishers Ltd.

2 4 6 8 10 7 5 3 1

Editorial office:
Polity Press
65 Bridge Street
Cambridge CB2 1UR, UK

Marketing and production:
Blackwell Publishers Ltd
108 Cowley Road
Oxford OX4 1JF, UK

Blackwell Publishers Inc.
238 Main Street
Cambridge, MA 02142, USA

ISBN 0–7456–1401–9
ISBN 0–7456–1402–7 (pbk)

A CIP catalogue record for this book is available from the British Library and
the Library of Congress.

Typeset in Palatino on 10/12pt
by Graphicraft Typesetters Ltd., Hong Kong
Printed in Great Britain by Hartnells Ltd., Bodmin, Cornwall

This book is printed on acid-free paper.

Contents

Acknowledgements

I would like to thank those who have supported me while writing and thinking about this book. I owe a great debt to Anthony Giddens, who supervised the Ph.D. thesis on which this book is based; his advice, support, criticism and encouragement have proved invaluable. Ernest Gellner, Salvador Giner, Joan Manuel Guinda, Jonathan Fletcher, Josep Llobera, Francesc Xavier Puig Rovira, Carles Salazar and María del Mar Serrano read parts of previous drafts and offered their comments and criticism.

The thesis which inspired this book could not have been written without the financial assistance provided by King's College (Cambridge), and the CIRIT (*Generalitat de Catalunya*). A scholarship from the British Council–La Caixa allowed me to come to Cambridge in the first instance to do a master's degree that turned into a first step towards the writing of my Ph.D.

Introduction

Nationalism is revealing itself in many parts of the world as an unexpected and powerful phenomenon. The re-emergence of nationalism in Eastern Europe is sparking off nationalist feelings in several other countries. Yet within Western Europe nationalism is also currently of particular significance. The integrating force of the European Union contrasts sharply with the nationalist feelings of minorities included within European nation-states. The role of the European Union in relation to the political and cultural aspirations of ethnic minorities raises the question of whether these minorities would be able to develop and strengthen their identities within a new Europe. It also raises the issue of whether, on the contrary, the genesis of a European identity would erode particularism and difference.

I shall distinguish three major explanatory approaches to nationalism. The first focuses on the immutable character of the nation and I shall refer to it as essentialism. The second and the third are more abstract, theoretical approaches which involve going beneath the surface of nationalism to discover an underlying reality which is responsible for it. The demand for modernization, the development of new patterns of communication and the emphasis upon economic factors are among the elements the second approach draws upon. The third develops psychological theories associated with the need of individuals to be involved in a collectivity with which they can identify.

The essentialist conception is not really a theory of nationalism, but an interpretation often incorporated within nationalist symbols themselves. It stems from authors such as Herder, and from Romanticism. It considers the nation to be a natural, quasi-eternal entity created by

God. A particular language and culture embody the role each nation has to perform in history. Emphasis is placed on emotional and ideational aspects of the community rather than economic, social and political dimensions.

The second approach considers nationalism in terms of modernization. Gellner offers the most sophisticated account of nationalism within this framework. In his view, the economies of industrialized states depend upon a homogenizing high culture, mass literacy and an educational system controlled by the state. 'Industrial man', writes Gellner, 'can be compared with an artificially produced or bred species which can no longer breathe effectively in the nature-given atmosphere, but can only function effectively and survive in a new, specially blended and artificially sustained air or medium . . . It requires a specialized plant. The name for this plant is a national educational and communications system. Its only effective keeper and protector is the state.'[1]

Deutsch focuses on the development of internal communications within states as leading to the creation of a common sense of moral and political identity. He argues: 'in the political and social struggles of the modern age, nationality means an alignment of large numbers of individuals from the middle and lower classes linked to regional centres and leading social groups by channels of social communication and economic intercourse, both indirectly from link to link and directly with the centre.'[2]

Kedourie refers to nationalism as a doctrine involving a complex of interrelated ideas about the individual, society and politics, and he highlights the role of Western intellectuals in creating it. In his opinion, 'the inventors of the doctrine tried to prove that nations are obvious and natural divisions of the human race, by appealing to history, anthropology, and linguistics. But the attempt breaks down since, whatever ethnological or philological doctrine may be fashionable for the moment, there is no convincing reason why the fact that people speak the same language or belong to the same race should, by itself, entitle them to enjoy a government exclusively their own.'[3]

The economistic explanation is a theory developed within, but not restricted to, Marxist accounts of the national question. The most illuminating account of nationalism from a Marxist point of view produced in recent times is that put forward by Nairn. He understands nationalism as a product of the uneven development of regions within the world capitalist economy. Nairn refers to nationalism as an effect of the expansion of capitalism: 'As capitalism spread, and smashed the ancient social formations surrounding it, they always tended to fall apart along the fault-lines contained inside them. It is a matter of elementary truth that these lines were nearly always ones of nationality (although in certain well-known cases deeply established religious divisions could perform the same function).'[4]

The third approach is exemplified by Smith and Anderson who provide the most far-reaching theories about the significance of national identity and the emergence of national consciousness. Smith highlights the importance of national identity as the most potent and durable influence of current collective cultural identities. He argues that 'the need for collective immortality and dignity, the power of ethno-history, the role of new class structures and the domination of inter-state systems in the modern world, assure the continuity of national identity to command humanity's allegiances for a long time to come, even when other larger-scale but looser forms of collective identity emerge alongside national ones.'[5]

Anderson defines the nation as an 'imagined community', limited, sovereign and worthy of sacrifices. He writes: 'nationalism has to be understood by aligning it, not with self-consciously held political ideologies, but with large cultural systems that preceded it, out of which – as well as against which – it came into being.' Anderson points to the importance of the development of the printed word as the basis for the emergence of national consciousnesses.[6]

It is my contention that, although these accounts have made significant contributions to a fuller understanding of nationalism, each theory is deficient in certain crucial respects to explain the saliency of such a powerful contemporary phenomenon. I consider nationalism to be an ideology closely related to the rise of the nation-state and bound up with ideas about popular sovereignty and democracy brought about by the French and American Revolutions. The fragmentary nature of current approaches to nationalism originates from their inability to merge its two fundamental attributes: the political character of nationalism as an ideology defending the notion that state and nation should be congruent; and its capacity to be a provider of identity for individuals conscious of forming a group based upon a common culture, past, project for the future and attachment to a concrete territory. The power of nationalism emanates from its ability to engender sentiments of belonging to a particular community. Symbols and rituals play a major role in the cultivation of a sense of solidarity among the members of the group.

Central questions and structure

In the light of these observations, this book has three primary tasks. First, to analyse the implications of the absence of a systematic consideration of issues of nationalism in classical social theory. There are various reasons for this neglect: the methodological difficulties of defining, classifying and explaining nationalism, and the theoretical concerns generated by the European origins of sociology and its Eurocentric outlook.[7] Sociology, as Smith argues, arose in countries with a fairly firmly entrenched sense of nationality which was both clear-cut and dominant within the state apparatus and polity.

Second, to establish a distinction between 'state nationalism' and nationalism in 'nations without a state' and investigate how differences in access to power and resources impinge upon the unfolding of nationalism in both cases. In discussing this, I focus upon commonly neglected aspects of nationalism and argue that the distinction between classical nationalism and that of nations without a state is crucial to an understanding of the problems of legitimacy that stem from ideas of popular sovereignty and democracy in the contemporary world.

Third, to explore what I shall refer to as the 'dark side' of nationalism. The extreme complexity of nationalism springs from the radically different interpretations to which it can be subject. In certain cases nationalism is employed in association with xenophobia, racism, fascism and all sorts of violent behaviour against 'the others'. On other occasions, it refers to the legitimate aspiration of peoples willing to sustain and develop their culture and vindicate their right to self-determination.

In the opening chapter, the theory of nationalism and the nation-state is related to its origins in classical social theory, paying particular attention to the work of Treitschke, Marx, Durkheim and Weber. I seek to explain why the latter three failed to predict the importance that nationalism would achieve in the twentieth century. Despite the fact that Weber and Treitschke were nationalists, why did they not construct a theory of nationalism? I am justified, I believe, in selecting these authors from a diversity of others who could have been chosen from the early period of the development of social thought, because they – particularly Marx, Durkheim and Weber, of course – so heavily influenced the subsequent evolution of social theory. Thus I have concentrated upon their work in some detail, rather than trying to cover a larger number of thinkers more superficially. I shall not be interested *only* in the question of why none of them worked at a systematic interpretation of nationalism. All of these thinkers, including Treitschke, made significant contributions to the analysis of the modern state; and a view of the state is necessary to an understanding of the character of the nation-state as a specific organizational form. From this aspect, it is possible to draw upon their work in a more direct way. Indeed most current accounts of the modern state are indebted to ideas first elaborated by these authors.

The second and third chapters seek to redress social theory's neglect of nationalism and provide answers to two key questions: what is the relation between nationalism and the nation-state?; and, what are the links between nationalism, culture and identity? In so doing I analyse the political character of nationalism and its relation to the concepts of legitimacy, citizenship and ideology. I then look at the creation and development of national identity and its relation to culture. Here it is argued that the current unfolding of nationalism not only derives from a gulf between political and cultural processes, but also gains strength as other criteria of group membership (such as class) weaken or recede. My thesis is that national solidarity responds to a need for identity of an eminently symbolic nature, in so far as it provides roots based on culture and a common past, as well as offering a project for the future.

Chapter four studies the association of a certain type of nationalism with racism and concentrates upon the use of nationalism in the fascist discourse. In these cases the relation between 'insiders' and 'outsiders' is characterized by a rejection and hostility that, on many occasions, leads to violence. The supremacy of one group above others, the prominence of leadership, the role of gender and the enormous capacity to mobilize large populations are some of the aspects of fascism analysed in this section.

In chapter five I emphasize once more the distinctiveness of the nationalism of nations without a state in comparison with that of the nation-state. I offer a detailed examination of the different political scenarios in which nations without a state are placed and study the processes leading to the emergence of 'national awareness'. This chapter then goes on to investigate the strategies used by national minorities in surviving repression and resisting the homogenizing policies frequently employed by the state. It also explores the options faced by national minorities confronted with a choice between fighting for independence – and so facilitating a possible reshaping of the nation-state system – or remaining within large states in which they can expect mutual coexistence.

The sixth chapter considers the emergence of nationalism in Third

World countries and focuses upon the African case. This section involves a study of the role played by nationalism as a liberation movement fighting for independence in the colonial era, and it also advances an analysis of the new uses and content of nationalism once independence was achieved. The final chapter explores the impact of modernity and globalization upon contemporary nationalism. Here, discussion of the possibilities for the emergence of a 'global identity' leads to a consideration of nationalism as a 'local' reaction to globalization. A further element taken into account is the recent expansion of Islamic Fundamentalism as a movement that is hostile to the Western view of modernity and sustains a dialectic relation with globalization.

To begin with, I turn to the issue of the discussion of nationalism in classical social theory. The ideas of Treitschke provide an appropriate starting-point, given his influence upon both Durkheim and Weber – even though both, particularly Durkheim, were heavily critical of his views. Treitschke cannot be regarded as a leading sociological thinker, in spite of his enormous influence in the Germany of his day. His ideas sound archaic today – a sign of how things have moved on – but were of key significance as a foil for the development of ideas about the state, the nation and nationalism in classical social thought.

1

Nationalism in Classical Social Theory

Heinrich von Treitschke

The state

Treitschke defines the state as 'the people legally united as an independent power'. By the people he understands 'a plural number of families permanently living together'.[1] In his view, the state is always above individuals and has the right to be omnipotent over them. The state is power. The power of the state is exerted in two major ways. First, the state is the 'supreme moralizing and humanizing agency'. In Treitschke's view, no moral law exists for the state. Rather, it is the state itself that establishes the law in its own domain and requires loyal obedience from individuals. The state has no commitments. There is no authority above it. He argues that every nation will have a special code of morality depending upon the particular needs of the state and the different features of its citizens. Hence the state is a moral community, one of several ideas which Treitschke derives from Aristotle.

Second, the state exerts its power through war. Treitschke defines the state as the only entity capable of maintaining a monopoly of violence when he writes, 'the right of arms distinguishes the state from all other forms of corporate life.'[2] The state is founded upon the possession of territory.[3] As we shall see, territory and violence are two crucial elements later incorporated by Weber into his own definition of the state. Treitschke argues that international treaties may indeed become more frequent, but a decisive tribunal of nations is impossible. The appeal to arms will be valid until the end of history and therein lies the sacredness of war,[4] which he regards as one of the normal activities of nations: 'The grandeur of history lies in the perpetual conflict of nations, and it is simply foolish to desire the suppression of their rivalry.'[5] Treitschke predicts that wars will become fewer and shorter, but, in his view, it would be a fallacy to infer from this that they could ever cease.[6] He neither envisages nor wishes a peaceful future for humanity. Thus, for him:

> War is political science par excellence. Over and over again has it been proved that it is only in war a people becomes in very deed a people. It is only in the common performance of heroic deeds for the sake of the fatherland that a nation becomes truly and spiritually united.[7]

'War is a sharp medicine for national disunion and waning patriotism,'[8] he adds; 'it is political idealism that demands war.'[9] War fulfils three major functions: it settles quarrels which 'must' arise between independent states; it is a remedy against national disunion; and it is a means to create new states. Treitschke emphasizes that if a state loses its independence, it ceases to be a state. Consequently, the chief tasks of the state which derive directly from its power involve the administration of justice, the creation of a moral law, and war. To be able to exert its power, the state must have sufficient material resources for self-defence and absolute sovereignty.

The relation between the individual and the state is determined by the superiority Treitschke confers on the latter. Following Aristotle, he argues that the interests of the community are above those of the individual:

> The individual must forget his own ego and feel himself a member of the whole; he must recognise what a nothing his life is in comparison with the general welfare[10] . . . The individual must sacrifice himself for a higher community of which he is a member; but the state is itself the highest in the external community of men.[11]

Treitschke requires an absolute surrender of the individual to the state and does not contemplate the possibility of revolution or even disagreement: 'the individual should feel himself a member of his state, and as such have courage to take its errors upon him.'[12] He goes on to say that 'states do not arise out of the people's sovereignty, but they are created against the will of the people; the state is the power of the stronger race which establishes itself.'[13] The dimension of the individual is not limited to his or her membership of the state; Treitschke recognizes an 'immortal and individual soul in every man' but he restricts human freedom to 'the right to think freely concerning God and divine things'. However, he declares that it is impractical for the state to tolerate different religions because 'the unity of the state is impossible when its subjects are divided between radically different religions.'[14]

In the work of Treitschke, therefore, we find a generalized idea of the state as a supreme entity guided 'not by emotions, but by calculating, clear experience of the world'.[15] The state 'protects and embraces the life of the people, regulating it externally in all directions'.[16]

On German unification

Treitschke's position on German unification is mainly expounded in *Bundesstaat und Einheitsstaat* (1864). In his view the German empire is based upon the existence of a dominant state, Prussia, and he envisages the creation of a 'Greater Germany' under Prussian leadership. In order to achieve this, Prussia should conquer the smaller states and incorporate them. Treitschke's Machiavellianism is evident since both he and Machiavelli agree that the interest of the nation must be set above the ordinary obligations of law and morality. Yet there is a difference between them; while Machiavelli sees no hope in any established dynasty and looks for a Prince 'who will begin at the beginning' (Cesare Borgia), Treitschke sees in the Hohenzollerns a monarchy which may shortly become strong enough to guide the process of German unification. Treitschke writes: 'I realize that for Germany there is only one hope of salvation, namely, a united and indivisible monarchy . . . Prussia, then, has no choice. She must triumph with the help of the German people.'[17]

Treitschke analyses three different possibilities for German unification: *Staatenbund, Bundesstaat* and *Einheitsstaat*. The first refers to the foundation of a Confederation of German States for mutual defence, one that lacks central institutions and which would leave the sovereignty of single states untouched. The *Bundesstaat* would imply the creation of an institution analogous to that of the United States of America, with a central executive, legislature and judiciary. The central government would be superior to that of the integrant states and have an unflexible constitution. This second option was rejected by him, but was finally adopted in the constitution of the German empire.

Treitschke presented the *Einheitsstaat* as 'the only valid alternative', involving the annihilation of the governments of smaller German states and the establishment of a unitary state in the form of an expanded Prussia. In 1864 he wrote:

> Every Prussian must feel it to be quite right that the best political institutions should be extended to the rest of Germany; and every reasonable non-Prussian must find cause for rejoicing that Prussia has brought the name of Germany into honour once again. The conditions are such that the will of the Empire can in the last instance be nothing else than the will of the Prussian state.[18]

Treitschke's relevance stems from the fact that he was one of the most influential figures of his time and profoundly affected the views of both Weber and Durkheim. The ideas he defended throughout his work, and expounded in his renowned, crowded lectures, influenced two generations of German academics: those who witnessed the unification of Germany and those who envisaged the formation of the Weimar Republic. We shall now move on to consider Treitschke's views on nationalism, which he discusses primarily under the rubric of patriotism.

On nationalism

For Treitschke, 'genuine patriotism is the consciousness of co-operating with the body-politic, of being rooted in ancestral achievements and of transmitting them to descendants.'[19] He appeals to a common historical past as one of the constituent features of patriotism. Consciousness and co-operation are key words in grasping his conception. 'To be conscious of' means 'to be aware of' and in the context of patriotism this means that individuals 'know' that they are, and 'are conscious of' being, members of a given community. It is not simply a matter of 'living in' a particular state; individuals should be 'conscious of belonging to' a particular group. Furthermore, patriotism requires active participation. Treitschke writes about the consciousness 'of co-operating'. This is a basic concept within his framework since it establishes that individuals are not merely members of a community, but are involved in a process. They are stewards of that other constituent feature of patriotism he appeals to, their common past. This relationship between the individual and the state provides the basis for the quasi-religious assertions he makes in discussing national honour:

Here the high moral ideal of national honour is a factor handed down from one generation to another, enshrining something positively sacred, and compelling the individual to sacrifice himself to it. This ideal is above all price and cannot be reduced to pounds, shilling and pence.[20]

Treitschke points to two powerful forces working in history: the tendency of every state to amalgamate its population, in speech and manners, into one single unity, and the impulse of every vigorous nationality to construct a state of its own.[21] If we add to this the fact that, for him, nation and state should coincide, it is easy to understand why he thought that Prussia should be the 'unifying agent' which all the other states should join in order to create a Greater Germany. He adds: 'only brave nations have a secure existence, a future, a development; cowardly nations go to the wall, and rightly so.'[22]

Treitschke stresses that 'the unity of the state should be based on nationality. The legal bond must at the same time be felt to be a natural bond of blood-relationship – either real or imaginary blood-relationship (for on this point nations labour under the most extraordinary delusions).'[23] In his view, patriotism is the consciousness of being rooted in ancestral achievements. However, he recognizes that 'nationality is not a settled and permanent thing'.[24] When talking about nationalism and patriotism, he focuses primarily on sizeable, powerful nation-states. Treitschke argues that 'the great state has the noble capacity . . . Only in great states can there be developed that genuine national pride which is the sign of the moral efficiency of a nation.' Not only does he refer to the moral 'grandeur' of large states, he also attributes cultural supremacy to them: 'All real masterpieces of poetry and art arose upon the soil of great nationalities'.[25] We should bear in mind that for Treitschke '*Staat ist Macht*', and a larger state means a more powerful one. He discounts the fact that a large state is by no means necessarily 'nobler' than and 'culturally superior' to a smaller one. That larger states have the power to impose their own way of thinking, present themselves as 'superior states', and promote their art and culture is taken for granted. However, as a historian, Treitschke was aware of the rise and fall of states through different periods, and this led him to leave open the possibility of success for small nationalities: 'The nations themselves are something living and growing. No one can say with absolute certainty when the small nationalities will decay internally and shrivel up, or when, on the other hand, they will exhibit an unexpected vital energy.'[26]

The superiority of Western culture, in Treitschke's view, derives from the fact that Western Europe 'has larger compact ethnological masses, while the East is the classic soil for the fragments of nations'.[27] He describes the nineteenth century as a period in which 'a man thinks of himself in the first place as a German or a Frenchman, or whatever his nationality may be, and only in the second place as a member of the whole human race'.[28] In Treitschke's view, the explosion of nationalism during his lifetime was a 'natural revulsion against the world-empire of Napoleon. The unhappy attempt to transform the multiplicity of European life into the arid uniformity of universal sovereignty has produced the exclusive sway of nationality as the dominant political idea. Cosmopolitanism has receded too far.'[29] He writes:

> The idea of a World-state is odious; the ideal of one state containing all mankind is no ideal at all . . . the whole content of civilisation cannot be realised in a single state . . . All peoples, just like individual men, are one-sided, but in the very fullness of this one-sidedness the richness of the human race is seen. Every people has therefore the right to believe that certain powers of the divine reason display themselves in it at their highest.[30]

To confirm this argument Treitschke notes that 'every nation over-estimates itself', and more importantly that 'without this feeling of itself, *the nation* would also lack the consciousness of being a com-munity'.[31] But what will be the future of nationalism in a world where, for the first time in history, it is possible to speak of a worldwide culture? A standard response to this sort of question is to seek to demonstrate that national particularities will disappear in favour of a more general and global culture. Treitschke approaches this issue in a different way, arguing that:

> The notion that a universally-extended culture will finally displace national customs by customs for all mankind, and turn the world into a cosmopolitan primitive hash has become a common-place . . . If a nation has the power to preserve itself and its nationality through the merciless race-struggle of history, then every progress in civilisation will only develop more strikingly its deeper national peculiarities.[32]

Power is a recurrent theme in Treitschke's thought. But in practical terms, what exactly does it mean for the nation 'to have the power to preserve itself'? To what extent is it possible for a nation to preserve itself in a world where globalization processes are becoming more and more compelling? Does the assertion that 'only' powerful nations will be able to preserve their 'national peculiarities' mean that only a very few nations will 'preserve themselves', while the rest will be fully absorbed or at least 'culturally assimilated' by their more powerful companions? For now I shall leave these questions open, but I shall return to them in a later discussion of the link between nationalism and globalization.

Karl Marx

Nationalism and the bourgeoisie

In the *Communist Manifesto*, Marx describes the history of human society in terms of class struggle: 'Freeman and slave, patrician and plebeian, lord and serf, guild master and journeyman, in a word, oppressor and oppressed, stood in constant opposition to one another.'[33] The struggle of 'oppressors and oppressed' ends either in a revolutionary reconstitution of society – where, prior to socialism, the 'oppressed' become 'oppressors' – or in the common ruin of the contending classes. Contemporary society is divided into two great classes, directly facing each other: bourgeoisie and proletariat. For Marx, social classes are the proper actors in the historical process. Local and national developments form only a part, and an admittedly insignificant one, unless a nation happens to find itself at the head of the progress of all humanity during a certain turning point in world history. This is a crucial issue in understanding why Marx pays so little attention to nationalism. For him, nations, states and cities need to be studied and evaluated within the context and from the perspective of their place in class relations and in the class struggle occurring on a global scale.

In Marx's view, bluntly stated, nationalism is an expression of bourgeois interests. But as Bloom rightly points out, 'the bourgeois "fatherland" did not refer to the country's potentialities for progress or to the nation regarded democratically, but to the aggregate of institutions, customs, laws, and ideas which sanctified the right to property on a considerable scale.'[34] Marx writes: 'The bourgeoisie conveniently assumed that the "nation" consisted only of capitalists. The country was therefore "theirs".'[35] He considers the nationalistic claims aimed at creating a unified Germany out of the existing thirty-eight states as bourgeois. In his *Contribution to the Critique of Hegel's Philosophy of Right*, he denounces the backwardness of Germany as a fundamental fact. For him, such backwardness revealed itself in the poverty of political aspirations and intellectual outlook of the German bourgeoisie. He considered France and Great Britain to be in a more advanced stage of development and, for that reason, he saw the abolition of the capitalist system in these two countries as something imminent. In contrast, he regarded Germany as a country in which a capitalist system was yet to be fully realized. However, German backwardness was not all-pervasive. Germany had developed the most up-to-date philosophical framework and should work to put its economy and policy at the same level. Marx advocated a revolution in Germany that would aim not only to elevate it to the same stage as the other most advanced nations of the West, but also to enable it to perform a task which even these nations had yet to accomplish: the liberation of individuals as human beings, rather than of Germans as Germans. But how could this liberation be possible if Germany did not have a class capable of acting as 'a negative representative of society', as the bourgeoisie did in France? Was there a real possibility for emancipation in Germany? In answer to this question, Marx comments:

> In Germany no type of enslavement can be abolished unless all enslavement is destroyed. Germany, which likes to get to the bottom of things, can only make a resolution which upsets the whole order of things. The emancipation of the German is the emancipation of the human being. Philosophy is the head of this emancipation and the proletariat is its heart. Philosophy can only be realised by the abolition of the proletariat, and the proletariat can only be abolished by the realisation of philosophy.
>
> When all the inner conditions ripen, the day of German resurrection will be proclaimed by the crowing of the Gallic cock.[36]

However, Marx was aware that in Germany the proletariat was only beginning to emerge under the impact of industrial development. He was conscious of the relative youth and weakness of the German proletariat, but he was also optimistic about the role it might play:

> When the proletariat announces the dissolution of the existing social order, it only declares the secret of its own existence, for it is the effective dissolution of this order . . . Just as philosophy finds its material weapons in the proletariat; so the proletariat finds its intellectual weapons in philosophy. And once the lightning of thought has penetrated deeply into this virgin soil of the people, the Germans will emancipate themselves and become men.[37]

Marx did not write in favour of an 'emancipation of Germany' that would realize German nationalist goals in the form of a single state. Instead he sought the abolition of the state. Marx's draft of an article on F. List's *Das nationale System der politischen Ökonomie* provides a detailed elaboration of his position on the 'German Question' and complements the ideas expounded in his *Contribution to a Critique of Hegel's 'Philosophy of Right'*. In his *Critique of List*, Marx views nationalism as a bourgeois ideology and List as its representative.[38] He rejects List's attempt to find a national road to capitalism and dismisses the possibility of communism in one country. Furthermore, Marx considers that both capitalism and communism are worldwide systems. List, unlike Marx, bases his entire argument on the recognition of nations as the basic units into which the human race is divided, and argues that nations develop by passing through clearly definable stages.

The German bourgeoisie appealed to 'nationality', but to Marx 'nationality' was a fraud. He argues that the bourgeoisie as a class has a common interest, and 'this community of interest, which is directed against the proletariat inside the country, is directed against the bourgeois of other nations outside the country. This the bourgeois calls his nationality.'[39] However, Marx does not specify how and why it should be possible for some bourgeois to agree on a common interest against other bourgeois; nor does he consider why the basis for union and separation should be German nationality.

Nationalism and the proletariat

In *The German Ideology* Marx refers to the proletariat as a class completely unlike any other, 'the class which no longer counts as a class in society, is not recognised as a class, and is in itself the expression of the dissolution of all classes, nationalities, etc., within present society.'[40] For Marx this is the result of modern industrial labour and modern subjection to capital in a world led by the bourgeoisie. In this world the proletariat has no property, becomes alienated and is a mere instrument in the hands of the bourgeois. The proletarian spends his or her life working, producing goods and benefits for the bourgeoisie. The more he or she works, the more impoverished he or she becomes. Marx denounced this situation and thought that the proletariat all over the world would be able to unite and fight. They would be the 'motor of history', and had nothing to lose in the struggle since they did not possess anything. In the *Communist Manifesto* he writes: 'The working men have no country . . . National differences and

antagonisms between peoples are daily more and more vanishing.'[41]
The present conditions of labour and subjection to capital which are
'the same in England as in France, in America as in Germany, have
stripped the proletariat of every trace of national character'.[42]

> The nationality of the worker is neither French, nor English, nor German, it is labour, free slavery, self-huckstering. His government is neither French, nor English, nor German, it is capital. His native air is neither French, nor German, nor English, it is factory air. The land belonging to him is neither French, nor English, nor German, it lies a few feet below the ground.[43]

Engels, in a letter to 'the working classes of Great Britain', expresses
the same viewpoint. He addresses the working classes as if they were
not English. Instead he emphasizes the common qualities of being

> members of the great and universal family of Mankind, who know their interest and that of all the human race to be the same. And as such, as members of this family of One and Indivisible Mankind, as Human Beings in the most emphatical meaning of the word, as such I, and many others on the Continent, hail your progress in every direction and wish you speedy success.[44]

The working class, as subject of history and social actor *par excellence*,
should only think in international terms: 'National one-sidedness and
narrow-mindedness become more and more impossible.'[45] Following
this line of argument, in his *Account of his speech on Mazzini's attitude
towards the International* Engels stresses: 'The International recognises
no country; it desires to unite, not dissolve. It is opposed to the cry for
Nationality, because it tends to separate people from people, and is
used by tyrants to create prejudices and antagonism.'[46] Marx argues
that the distinctive feature of the communists when compared with
other working-class parties is that, 'in the national struggles of the
proletarians of the different countries, the communists point out
and bring to the front the common interests of the entire proletariat,
independent of all nationality.'[47]

Nationalism and proletarian revolution

1848/49 seems to herald a major modification of Marx and Engels'
original stand on nationalism, in that they supported the national
causes of the 'historic' or 'great' nations such as Hungary, Poland and

Germany, all of which sought to establish large, stable national states. Nationalism appeared to be compatible with a proletarian revolution in as much as large states would make it easier for the proletariat to advance its class goals. Marx and Engels voiced their hostility towards the aspirations of 'non-historic nationalities' such as the smaller Slavic nations, particularly the Czechs. In an article published in 1852 in the *New York Daily Tribune*, Engels, under Marx's name, referred to the high culture, the high development in science and industry of Germany, compared with that of the Slavs. He argued that the Slavs were living in a condition of backwardness and that their way of life was being dissolved 'by contact with a superior German culture'.

In 1872 Engels recognized one nationality in particular: the Irish. When Great Britain tried to bring the Irish sections under the jurisdiction of the British Federal Council, he argued: 'The Irish form, to all intents and purposes, a distinct nationality of their own, and the fact that they use the English language can not deprive them of the right, common to all, to have an independent national organisation within the International.'[48] Engels makes clear that a nation should be free from its conquerors because only then can the workers think in international terms about a world working-class solidarity. Internationalism must not be used as an excuse to justify and perpetuate the dominion of the conqueror.

> If members of a conquering nation called upon the nation they had conquered and continued to hold down to forget their specific nationality and position, to 'sink national differences' and so forth, that was not Internationalism, it was nothing else but preaching to their submission to the yoke, and attempting to justify and to perpetuate the dominion of the conqueror under the cloak of Internationalism.[49]

Accordingly, true Internationalism must necessarily be based upon a distinctly national organization:

> The Irish, as well as other oppressed nationalities, could enter the Association only as equals with the members of the conquering nation, and under protest against the conquest . . . The Irish sections, therefore, not only were justified, but even under the necessity to state in the preamble to their rules that their first and most pressing duty, as Irishmen, was to establish their own national independence.[50]

In *The Communist Manifesto*, Marx points out that the struggle of the proletariat with the bourgeoisie is 'at first a national struggle', emphasizing that 'the proletariat of each country must, of course, first of all settle matters with its own bourgeoisie.'[51] He also suggests that, 'the proletariat must first of all acquire political supremacy, must rise to be the leading class of the nation, must constitute itself the nation, it is, so far, itself national, though not in the bourgeois sense of the word.'[52] Further, in the *Critique of the Gotha Programme*, Marx argues that, 'it is altogether self-evident that, to be able to fight at all, the working class must organise itself at home as a class and that its own country is the immediate arena of its struggle.'[53] In saying this, he does not attempt to formulate any kind of nationalist claim. Marx regarded the working class as an international class to be united above national affiliation, and envisaged the abolition of the state. It is precisely this kind of ambiguous formulation which makes it possible to specify compatibilities between Marxism and nationalism. Marx's internationalism was not an attempt to eliminate cultural differences among societies, or to favour uniformity. Rather, the assumption of large societies seemed to him a more effective starting point for the establishment of an harmonious world. He was an internationalist, not only in the sense that he was advocating a system of co-operative world relations, but more specifically in conceiving of that system as the outcome or function of the friendly interaction of large nations which were organized harmoniously within. In my view, Marx's goal was not the removal of all national distinctions, but the abolition of the sharp economic and social inequalities derived from capitalism, and the establishment of a world in which the emancipation of all individuals as human beings would be possible.

Marx did not present a theory of nationalism for three main reasons. First, according to him, in class societies the prevailing ideas of any epoch are the ideas of the ruling class. It follows from this proposition that the diffusion of ideas is heavily dependent upon the distribution of economic power in society. In this latter sense, ideology constitutes part of the social 'superstructure': the prevalent ethos at any given time is one which provides legitimation of the interests of the dominant class. Thus, the relations of production, via the mediation of the class system, compose the real foundation on which emerges a legal and political superstructure and to which definite forms of social consciousness correspond. However, Marx does not postulate an unvarying connection between these two modes in which consciousness is moulded by social praxis. An individual or group may develop ideas which are partially at variance with the prevalent views of their age, but these ideas will not come into prominence unless they articulate with interests held by the dominant class, or with those of a class established in a position from which to challenge the existing authority structure. Marx could see nothing but the economic self-interest of the bourgeoisie in German nationalist claims. He was mainly concerned with the study of the economic relations in society because he thought that to be able to introduce changes in the superstructure one should be able to change the relations of production and the distribution of economic power. This is one of the reasons which explains why Marx did not pay much attention to the study of nationalism: his primary concern was the study of the economy.

Second, Marx's understanding of history as the history of class struggle implies that a proletarian revolution should follow a bourgeois one and impose the dictatorship of the proletariat as a stage on the road towards a communist society. Marx envisaged a stateless society free from class struggle as a long-term goal. This process seems to leave no room for nationalism, since nationalism's main goal is the creation of a state, not its abolition. However, if we consider Marx and Engels' position on Irish nationality, it is possible to find a place for nationalism, at least in the sense that a country needs to be free from its conquerors before engaging in the class struggle. Marx also writes that the working class has first of all to settle matters with 'its own bourgeoisie', and although he never explains this, it would appear that, at least in the provisional but necessary stages before reaching the 'communist society', a certain version of nationalism and Marxism could form a unity, especially since the end of this provisional period was not fixed.

The third reason for Marx giving scant attention to nationalism lies in his notion that neither capitalist relations of production, nationality, nor religion should obstruct the liberation of people as human beings. The proletariat should transcend national identities and be able to recognize itself as 'part of the big family of Mankind'.

Nationalism and Marxism: similarities and differences

It is possible to find some similarities between nationalism and Marxism, similarities that have contributed to the union of these two forms of ideology in different countries, especially after Marx.[54] Nationalism and Marxism are both what Smith calls 'salvation movements'. They describe the present situation as an oppressive one, in which individuals live alienated lives (Marxism) or have lost their identity (nationalism).

For nationalism, the tyrant is the 'alien coloniser', the 'invading enemy' (imperialism, if we refer to Third World countries). For Marxism, the tyrant is the bourgeois capitalist. Both sorts of oppression entail uniformity, slavery and alienation; present social and political structures being polarized around conflicting interests and values. Nationalism and Marxism each define an inner, hidden corruption. Nationalists lament the loss of belonging and inner harmony of a submerged nation, a condition that results not – as for Marxists – from alienated labour, but from a breakdown in continuity with the community's past. Marxists denounce a double aspect of alienation, the concrete and the philosophical. The former reflects the situation of the proletarian labourer in his or her work situation (the objectification of labour), but beyond this concrete alienation there is also a more generalized form which includes every projection of individuals' thoughts and activities that become separate and external to them. What is clear to both Marxists and nationalists is that the current situation needs to be changed, and that they are willing to change it. As a consequence, both movements defend the need for the regeneration of individuals and the return to an authentic state of being where human self-realization is possible.

Nationalism and Marxism share the myth of a final era of justice and freedom, although they view the past in different ways. Nationalism seeks inspiration from the past in order to restore national identity and free the nation from its oppressors. Marxism accepts a dialectical conception of historical development in which the past is accepted in order to transcend it and advance through the stages of history.

Three more common characteristics can be discerned. First, both nationalism and Marxism find the proper arena of their struggle in the modern nation-state. Second, as a consequence of their ideas about regeneration and the need to overcome the present situation, both are profoundly activist social movements. Although they rely on mass mobilization, both also entrust groups of intellectuals with the task of leading the movement. From a Marxist point of view, the 'intelligentsia' will be charged with the study and diffusion of ideology; from a nationalistic position, this elite of intellectuals will claim privileged knowledge of the authentic origins of the community, which will enable them to fight for the defence of national identity and to teach the population about the distinctive parts of their culture that have disappeared as a consequence of alien oppression. Third, there is the union of Marxism and nationalism in some countries as the idea-system supporting anti-colonial movements. The following general conditions for its success can be highlighted: the perception of the community or area as peripheral in wealth and power, the establishment of a weak, ineffective government after independence and the threat of an external intrusion in economic or military terms. As Smith mentions, two types of 'power dependency' are particularly pertinent to the rise of Marxist nationalisms: a long-delayed independence from colonialism; and a nominal independence which is economic-ally and sometimes militarily dependent upon neighbouring or dis-tant powers.

To summarize, some of the main differences between nationalism and Marxism are: first, while nationalism gives primary emphasis to culture, Marxism traces back every phenomenon to its economic roots; second, Marxists locate their enemy in the capitalist without consider-ing his or her nationality, while for nationalists, the enemy is those who corrupt and oppress the purity of the nation; and finally, the two forms of ideology espouse a different interpretation of the past. As I have mentioned, Marxists accept the past in order to transcend it, while nationalists seek inspiration from the past in order to link it with the present, restoring the original features of the national character.

Emile Durkheim

The state

Durkheim distinguishes between what he calls 'political society' and the 'state'. While the latter refers to 'the agents of the sovereign au-thority', the former refers to 'the complex group of which the State is the highest organ'.[55] He also separates the state itself from secondary organizations, such as the law, the army and the Church – where there is a national church – in the immediate field of the state's control. According to Durkheim, the state can be defined as a group of officials sui generis, within which representations and acts of volition involving the collectivity are worked out, although they are not the product of the collectivity. It is not accurate to say that the state embodies the collective consciousness, for that goes beyond the state at every point. The representations that derive from the state are characterized by their higher degree of consciousness and reflection. The state does not execute anything; rather, it requires action to be taken. Its main function is to think in order to guide collective conduct. 'The state is above all a means of reflection . . . it is intelligence taking the place of obscure instinct.'[56]

In trying to establish the ends normally pursued by the state,

Durkheim criticizes both the individualistic theory defended by Spencer and the classical economists; and also Kant, Rousseau and the 'Spiritualistic school' (what Durkheim calls the 'mystic solution') set up by Hegel. The individualistic theory defines the state as an agent whose task is to watch over the maintenance of individual rights. Likewise, many thinkers have held that the prerogative of the state should be limited to administering a wholly negative justice; that is, the state's role has to be progressively limited to the prevention of unlawful trespass of one individual over another and the maintenance, on behalf of each person, of a sphere to which human beings have a right solely because they are what they are. Such authors attribute the great number of prerogatives the state had in the past to the insufficient stage of civilization reached by these societies. Durkheim argues that this theory does not agree with the facts, since the functions of the state tend to multiply and gain relevance. In Durkheim's view, the state has an inclination to expand its own scope.

'Mystic theory', in contrast, argues that every society has an aim that is superior to individual ones and is unrelated to them. It is the state's task to pursue this truly social aim, whilst individuals should be an instrument for putting into effect plans they have neither arranged nor are concerned about. Durkheim notes that this argument is enjoying a kind of revival due to 'the current confusion in ideas', and points out that in France 'there are those who throw themselves in despair back on the opposite faith and, renouncing the cult of the individual which was enough for our fathers, they try to revive the cult of the City-State in a new guise.'[57]

The relation between the individual and the state

The relation between the individual and the state has changed throughout the course of history. In Durkheim's view, the only aim of the state, in the beginning, was to become increasingly powerful, while at the same time ignoring the needs and interests of the individual. The only valuable things were 'collective beliefs', 'collective aspirations' and the traditions and symbols which expressed them: the individual was then completely absorbed into society. As we advance in history the individual becomes an object of moral consideration. Human beings obtain rights and the state recognizes their 'dignity'. 'Shall we find some people saying that the cult of the individual is a superstition of which we ought to rid ourselves? That would be to go against all the lessons of history: for as we read on, we find the human person tending to gain in dignity. There is no rule more soundly established.'[58] Following Durkheim's argument, this can lead to what may seem an antinomy: on the one hand, the spread and development of the state, and on the other, the development of individual rights. Durkheim rejects this possibility and stresses that our moral individuality is not antagonistic to the state; on the contrary, it is a product of it. The state, in his discourse, tends to reveal the nature of the individual. In *l'État* he writes: 'The state becomes stronger and more active as the individual becomes freer. It is the state that frees the individual.'[59] The state has created and organized individual rights: 'Man is only man to the degree that he is civilised.'[60] For Durkheim the essential function of the state is to free individuals. To accomplish this the state must permeate all secondary groups – family, trade, church, professional association and so on – which tend to absorb the personality of their members. 'The state', Durkheim writes, 'must therefore enter into the lives of the individuals, it must supervise and keep a check on the way they operate and to do this it must spread its roots in all directions.'[61]

Durkheim points out that the rights of the individual are in a state of evolution and it is not possible to set any boundaries on their course. However, he also stresses that the state's action can become despotic if there is nothing between the state and the individual. He writes in *Suicide* that the state's action can be useful only if it is diversified by a whole system of secondary organs.[62] Durkheim notes: 'The state too needs to be restrained by the totality of secondary forces that are subordinate to it but without which, like any unrestrained organism, it develops excessively and becomes tyrannical and forceful.'[63]

Features of the state

Durkheim makes a distinction between two types of state actions: external and internal. External action was pre-eminent in former times. Its main features were violent manifestations, aggression and war.[64]

Internal action is the main task of the state in modern societies. This action is primarily 'pacifique et morale', and should be understood as a result of the development of 'higher' societies. In his view, 'the state's attributions become ever more numerous and diverse as one approaches the highest types of society.'[65] In the context of this internal action, I shall discuss what Durkheim perceives to be the major functions of the state.

The state is not a mere spectator of social life; rather, it organizes and moralizes society.[66] The state is also the organ of social thought.[67]

Durkheim distinguishes two types: the first is derived from the collective mass of society and is diffused throughout that mass; the second is worked out in the state, has a particular structure and is centralized. He insists that the state thinks in order to guide collective conduct and not for the sake of thinking or building up doctrinal systems. In Durkheim's theory, the state has a positive human and non-transcendent role which is to free individuals. However, he notes that:

> a society made up of an extremely large mass of unorganised individuals, which an overgrown state attempts to limit and restrain, constitutes a veritable sociological monstrosity. For collective activity is always too complex to be capable of finding expression in the one single organ of the state.
>
> Moreover, the state is too remote from individuals, its connections with them too superficial and irregular, to be able to penetrate the depths of their consciousness and socialise them from within. This is why, when the state constitutes the sole environment in which men can fit themselves for the business of living in common, they inevitably 'contract out', detaching themselves from one another, and thus society disintegrates to a corresponding extent. A nation cannot be maintained unless, between the state and individuals, a whole range of secondary groups are interposed.[68]

The state tends to absorb all forms of activity which have a social character and is henceforth confronted by nothing but an unstable flux of individuals. In describing our moral situation, Durkheim emphasizes that human beings cannot become attached to higher aims and submit to a rule if they see nothing above them with which they can identify. To free individuals from all social pressure is to abandon them to themselves and demoralize them. Nowadays the state is compelled to assume functions for which it is ill-suited and which it has not been able to discharge satisfactorily: 'while the state becomes inflated and hypertrophied in order to obtain a firm enough grip upon individuals, but without succeeding, the latter, without mutual relationships, tumble over one another like so many liquid molecules, encountering no central energy to retain, fix and organise them.'[69] To remedy this, he suggests the formation of corporations, as definite institutions, each one becoming a moral individuality.

State and education

In Durkheim's view, education has a collective function: to adapt the child to the social environment in which he or she is destined to live:

'Education assures a sufficiently common body of ideas and feelings amongst citizens without which any society is impossible.'[70] As soon as education becomes an essential social function, it becomes a major concern for the state, and all that is educational must to some degree be subordinated to the state's actions. However, this does not necessarily mean that the state must monopolize schooling, although the state must have a stake in its control. According to Durkheim the role of the state is to distinguish the essential principles which form the basis of democratic ethics, to ensure they are taught in its schools, to instil them in children, and to see that they are accorded the respect due to them.

To complete Durkheim's theory of the state, two further aspects should be mentioned. Firstly, he considers war as largely a feature of the past and as something that is destined to disappear. For this reason, he proposes 'justice' as society's highest goal. In his view, the glory of the state no longer lies in the conquest of new territories but in a moral end: the expansion of justice within society.[71] Secondly, he sees the state as an agent that exists and develops in a milieu formed by the assembly of other states. Each state exists in relation to others, as it forms part of the international community. No state can exist in opposition to the rest of humanity. Durkheim stresses this point in *L'Allemagne au-dessus de tout*, describing the German mentality as an example of 'pathologie sociale'.[72] In his view, although the state is considered as something artificial, no state is strong enough to rule eternally against its citizens' will.[73]

State and democracy

Durkheim rejects the traditional theory of democracy, according to which the mass of the population 'participates' in the exercise of government. For him, this is a situation which is only possible in a society which is not a 'political society'. He points out that the state comes into existence by a process of concentration which detaches a certain group of individuals from the collective mass: government must be exercised by a minority of individuals. Democracy, therefore, must concern the relationship between the state and society. A democratic order exists when citizens are regularly informed of the activities of the state, and the state is aware of the sentiments and wishes of all sectors of the population.[74] In a democratic order, the role of the state does not simply express the sentiments held in a diffuse fashion among the population, but is often the origin of new ideas. In this context, the sphere of the state is larger than in other periods and society becomes more flexible. The occupational associations play a vital role in democratic societies, since they are the intermediaries between the state and the individual. Durkheim argues that secondary groups are essential if the state is not to oppress the individual; they are also necessary if the state is to be sufficiently free of the individual.[75] States become tyrannical if corporations do not exist.[76]

Drawing an organic analogy it is possible to argue, as Durkheim frequently did, that the state is the 'brain' – the conscious, directive centre – which operates via the intermediary organs within the complex nervous system of a differentiated society. A democratic order, he notes, enjoys the same relative superiority over other societies as the self-conscious being does over an animal whose behaviour is unreflective or instinctive. Durkheim places considerable emphasis upon the 'cognitive' as opposed to the 'active' significance of the state. The specific role of the democratic state is not to subordinate the individual to itself, but to provide for individuals' self-actualization, and this can only take place through membership of a society in which the state guarantees and advances the rights embodied in moral individualism.[77] Durkheim's main objection to democracy is that it is difficult to worship a legal order that can be easily changed if the majority of people so decide. In his view, the law should make explicit which are the natural relations among things. The law should be respected simply because it is 'good'.[78]

The state and religion

Durkheim considers society to be the source of religion. In *The Elementary Forms of the Religious Life*, he writes: 'religious forces are therefore human forces, moral forces.'[79] The principal object of religion is to act upon the moral life. Religion is the image of society; it reflects all its aspects, even the most vulgar and the most repulsive. The only characteristics shared equally by all religions are that they involve a certain number of people living together and usually show great intensity:

> In a general way, it is unquestionable that a society has all that is necessary to arouse the sensation of the divine in minds, merely by the power that it has over them; for to its members it is what a god is to his worshippers. In fact, a god is, first of all, a being whom men think of as superior to themselves, and upon whom they feel that they depend.[80]

Durkheim notes that, contrary to what would seem to be the case, even when religion appears to be entirely within the individual conscience, it is still created by society. He understands religion as an element of unity among believers and argues that when individual minds enter into a close relation and act upon each other a new kind of psychic life arises from their synthesis. Durkheim establishes a basic distinction between the sacred and the profane, stressing the role of the cult: 'in a word, it is necessary that we act, and that we repeat the acts thus necessary every time we feel the need of renewing their effects . . . It is the cult which gives rise to these impressions of joy, of interior peace, of serenity, of enthusiasm which are, for the believer, an experimental proof of his beliefs.'[81] Collective ideas and sentiments which make the unity and personality of a society need to be upheld and reaffirmed at regular intervals. Yet when Durkheim comments that: 'there is no essential difference between an assembly of Christians celebrating the principal dates of the life of Christ, or of Jews remembering the exodus from Egypt or the promulgation of the decalogue, and a reunion of citizens commemorating the promulgation of a new moral or legal system or some great event in the national life', he is not only describing a series of similarities between religious and civil ceremonies; he is emphasizing that both types of ceremonies do not differ 'either in their object, the results which they produce, or the processes employed to attain these results'.[82] Durkheim writes, referring to both religious and national rituals, that 'it is by uttering the same cry, pronouncing the same word, or performing the same gesture in regard to some object that they [the people] become and feel themselves to be in unison.'[83] The fact that religion, through ritual, shares common ideas, common obligations and common conduct means that it creates society in a more important sense than it is created by society. Ritual is not identical in all societies but, as Gellner points out, its underlying role remains the same:

> In the crazed frenzy of the collective dance around the totem, each individual psyche is reduced to a trembling suggestible jelly; the ritual then imprints the required shared ideas, the collective representations, on this malleable proto-social human matter. It thereby makes it concept-bound, constrained, and socially clubbable.[84]

Durkheim's theory of religion makes a decisive contribution to the understanding of nationalism since 'religion has given birth to all that is essential in society'.[85] For if 'in religious worship society adores its own camouflaged image, in a nationalist age', as Gellner notes, 'societies worship themselves brazenly and openly, spurning the camouflage.'[86] A further and more sophisticated dimension to Durkheim's theory of religion is added by Gellner's interpretation of it, when he writes that within Durkheim's framework, 'what makes us human and social is our capacity to be constrained by compulsive concepts, and the theory that the compulsion is instilled by ritual, and that ritual is the core of religion.'[87] If we replace the term religion by nationalism and take into account the fundamental role of rituals and symbols within the nationalist discourse, we can indeed apply to nationalism the capacity to restrain and instil cohesion within any one community as a means to obtain co-operation and communication. Gellner argues that in Durkheim's view, 'collective rituals inculcate shared compulsions, thereby quite literally humanising us. We co-operate because we think alike, and we think alike thanks to ritual.'[88]

Durkheim's theory of 'patriotism'

Durkheim's work does not contain an explicit theory of nationalism. In fact he does not use the term 'nationalism' but instead, like Treitschke, refers to 'patriotism'. He wrote little directly on nationalism, which means that we need to study his work carefully in order to piece together the comments on it which appear in various parts of his writings. According to Mauss, two manuscripts written by Durkheim dealing with nationalism during the First World War have since been lost: *Cours de Morale Théorique*, and *Cours de Morale civique et professionnelle*,[89] and it is therefore useful to construct a picture of Durkheim's views from other sources.

Durkheim distinguishes between 'nationality', 'state' and 'nation'. He defines 'nationality' as: 'human groups that are united by a community of civilisation without being united by a political bond'.[90] Durkheim uses the word 'nationality' to refer to large groups of individuals who do not constitute political societies, but possess a unity. He takes Poland and Finland as examples and stresses that they are not yet states but possess an historical reality. Nationalities, in Durkheim's theory, are either former states that have not given up the idea of reconstituting themselves, or states in the process of becoming. By 'state', he refers to 'the agents of sovereign authority',[91] thus implying the existence of a central power. By 'nation' he means a 'group that is both "state" and "nationality"'.[92]

Durkheim defines patriotism as 'a sentiment that joins the individual to the political society in so far as those who get to make it up feel themselves attached to it by a bond of sentiment'.[93] The 'patrie' (father-land) is the 'normal milieu which is indispensable to human life'.[94] Durkheim has a particular understanding of 'patriotism'. On the one hand, he identifies the 'patrie' as the highest organized society that exists and emphasizes that we cannot dispense with a 'patrie' since we cannot live outside of an organized society. On the other hand, he points out that 'national aims do not lie at the summit of the hierar-chy'; rather, 'it is human aims that are destined to be supreme'.[95] On this basis, he notes, it has sometimes been suggested that patriotism could be regarded simply as a phenomenon that would soon disap-pear. Durkheim recognizes that this idea is problematic: 'man is a moral being only because he lives within established societies . . . now patriotism is precisely the ideas and feelings as a whole which bind the individual to a certain state. If we suppose it to have weakened or to have ceased to exist, where is an individual to find this moral authority, whose curb is to this extent salutary?'[96]

Durkheim does not see 'patriotism' as a sentiment that will endure. In his view, a conflict has come about between 'equally high-minded kinds of sentiment – those we associate with a national ideal and the state that embodies it, and those we associate with the human ideal and mankind in general – in a word, between patriotism and world patriotism'.[97] Durkheim writes: 'Over and above the patrie there is yet another which is in the process of being formed, which envelops our national patrie. This is the European patrie or the human patrie.'[98] In his view, 'no matter how devoted men may be to their native land, they all today are aware that beyond the forces of national life there are others, in a higher region and not so transitory, for they are unrelated to conditions peculiar to any given political group and are not bound up with its fortunes.'[99]

It is not clear to Durkheim what attitude individuals should adopt in facing patriotism: 'to what extent should we desire this other kind of society [the human patrie]? Should we try to bring it about, to hasten its coming or, indeed, should we jealously maintain the inde-pendence of the present home-country to which we belong at all costs?'[100] This dichotomy is partially solved by Durkheim's identifica-tion of what he calls the 'national ideal' with the 'human ideal'. He argues that each state becomes an organ of the 'human ideal' in so far as it assumes that its main task is not to expand by extending its borders, but to increase the level of its members' morality. Therefore, societies should place their pride in becoming the best organized, having the best moral constitution, rather than in being the biggest or richest of all societies. This conception directly opposes that of Heinrich von Treitschke. In the context of the First World War, Durkheim wrote *L'Allemagne au-dessus de tout* and analysed the work of Treitschke as representative of the German collective mentality. Referring to Germany, Durkheim wrote:

> It is the need to declare itself, to feel that there is nothing superior to it. Impatience with all that is limited or dependent, in one word, the desire for power.... In order to justify itself, Germany has attributed to itself every kind of superiority, to make understandable this universal superiority, it has sought reasons in race, history and legend.[101]

In the pamphlet *Qui a voulu la guerre?*, Durkheim analyses the causes of the First World War and the attitudes of the different European countries involved, and adopts a French nationalist stance. He blames Germany and writes: 'There is not a single serious gesture of peace in Germany, there are only vain words.'[102] In Durkheim's view, 'Germany's culpability is obvious. Everything confirms it, and nothing can attenuate it . . . Furthermore, universal opinion is progressively less reluctant to blame the German government and make it responsible for the terrible calamity that our peoples are suffering today.'[103] When describing France's attitude he notes: 'In fact, France has fought to the end with all her energy to achieve peace . . . France's attitude towards the outside has always been irreproachably correct.'[104] Durkheim failed in his prediction when he considered 'patriotism' to be a transitory phenomenon: 'as we advance in evolution, we see the ideals men pursue breaking free of the local or ethnic conditions obtaining in a certain region of the world or a certain human group, and rising above all that is particular and so approaching the universal.'[105] In *Suicide*, he points out that 'today neither the commune, the department nor the province has enough ascendancy over us to exert this influence' and refers to them as 'conventional labels' devoid of meaning. According to him, 'local patriotism no longer exists nor can it exist.' Furthermore, 'it is impossible to artificially resuscitate a particularist spirit which no longer has any foundation.'[106] Durkheim stresses the same point in *The Division of Labour*, when he writes: 'an organisation based on territorial groupings becomes progressively weaker . . . geographical divisions are in the main artificial, and no longer arouse deep emotions within us. The provincial spirit has vanished beyond recall. "Parish pump" patriotism has become an anachronism that cannot be restored at will.'[107] History has proved Durkheim wrong in his prediction about the transitory character of patriotism. But it is obviously true that the global perception of the world we experience today opens the path towards 'human ideals' and radically transforms both the objectives and content of nationalism.

Max Weber

State and nation

Weber defines the state as 'a human community that (successfully) claims the *monopoly of the legitimate use of physical force* within a given territory.'[108] In his view, the state is considered the sole source of the 'right' to use violence. Hence, he concludes: '"politics" for us means striving to share power or striving to influence the distribution of power, either among states or among groups within a state.'[109] Weber's emphasis upon violence and territoriality in defining the state has clear roots in Treitschke's *Die Politik*. This explains Weber's faith in the intrinsic relation between power and the state, Machiavellianism and the importance of great leaders. However, he provides an account that is more far-reaching than Treitschke's. Weber has a keener under-standing of modern economic life and the importance and needs of the industrial proletariat, contrasting with Treitschke's struggle against the working class and social democracy. Weber's writings on the state offer the most sophisticated account of the four approaches included in this section. He not only attempts to establish a distinction between nation and state, but also connects his theory of values to notions of culture as a basis for the differences arising between nations. For only a state can ensure the survival of the many cultural values unique to nations.

The 'ethnic group' corresponds, in Weber's view, 'to one of the most vexing, since emotionally charged concepts: the *nation*, as soon as we attempt a sociological definition'.[110] He argues: 'We shall call "ethnic groups" those human groups that entertain a subjective belief in their common descent because of similarities of physical type or of customs or both, or because of memories of colonization and migration.'[111] Note that when Weber refers to 'ethnic groups', he mentions race and sim-ilarities of physical type as one among other elements that can be *subjectively* perceived as a common trait, but not as the 'only element'. In Weber's view, ethnic membership does not constitute a group; it only facilitates group formation of any kind, particularly in the polit-ical sphere. He stresses that it is primarily the political community, no matter how artificially organized, that inspires the belief in common ethnicity. This would imply that the state has a capacity to create a 'presumed identity' among its citizens. Furthermore, Weber's assertion that the belief in common ethnicity 'tends to persist even after the disintegration of the political community, unless drastic differences in the custom, physical type, or, above all, language exist among its members', could be regarded as an explanation for the continuity of the belief in common ethnicity felt by the population of territories such as Catalonia which had formed an independent political community in the past. Weber offers a broad definition of ethnicity and stresses that 'if rationally regulated action is not widespread, almost any association, even the most rational one, creates an overarching communal consciousness; this takes the form of a brotherhood on the basis of the belief in common ethnicity.'[112]

In particular, the political community can engender sentiments of likeness which will persist after its demise and will have an 'ethnic' connotation; but such an effect, Weber argues, is most directly created by the language group which is the bearer of a specific 'cultural possession of the masses' (*Massenkulturgut*) and makes mutual understanding (*Verstehen*) possible or easier. He points out that:

> Wherever the memory of the origin of a community by peaceful secession or emigration ('colony', *ver sacrum*, and the like) from a mother community remains for some reason alive, there undoubtedly exists a very specific and often extremely powerful sense of ethnic identity, which is determined by several factors: shared political memories or, even more importantly in early times, persistent ties with the old cult, or the strengthening of kinship and other groups, both in the old and the new community, or other persistent relationships.[113]

Weber does not mention nationalism, but he undoubtedly contributes to the understanding of it throughout his analysis of 'ethnic groups'. I shall emphasize the relevance of three points within his theory: the 'subjective character' of the ethnic group, the power of the political community to engender sentiments of likeness among its members, and the emotional character of ethnic bonds and their ability to create a sense of solidarity among group members.

'The concept of "nationality"', Weber argues, 'shares with that of the "people" (*Volk*) – in the "ethnic" sense – the vague connotation that whatever is felt to be distinctively common must derive from common descent.' But he immediately points out that 'persons who consider themselves members of the same nationality are often much less related by common descent than are persons belonging to different and hostile nationalities.' He notes that today, 'a shared common language is pre-eminently considered the normal basis of nationality.'[114] However, a common language, if relevant, is also insufficient to sustain a sense of national feeling *(Nationalgelfühl)*. In Weber's view, the significance of language is 'necessarily increasing along with the democratisation of state, society, and culture. Above all, the language, and that means the literature based upon it, is the first and for the time being the only cultural value at all accessible to the masses who ascend toward participation in culture.'[115]

Weber regards the nation as closely related to prestige interests. He notes that the earliest and most energetic manifestations of the idea of the nation contained the legend of a providential 'mission', one facilitated by the cultivation of the superiority, or at least the peculiarity, of the culture values of the group set off as a nation. In this context, it will be the task of intellectuals 'to propagate the "national idea", just as those who wield power in the polity provoke the idea of the state'.[116]

The concept of 'nation' undoubtedly means, above all, that one may expect from certain groups of individuals a specific sentiment of solidarity in the face of other groups. For Weber, national solidarity among people speaking the same language may be just as easily rejected as accepted. Instead, he suggests that solidarity may be linked to memories of a common political destiny. The causal components that lead to the emergence of a national sentiment may vary greatly, and, in Weber's view, common political destinies have first to be considered.

He defines the nation as a community of sentiment which would adequately manifest itself in a state of its own. Therefore nationality is not a sociologically distinct concept for Weber; it ought to be defined not from the standpoint of common qualities that establish the national community, but solely from the goal of an independent state. Weber explains that 'a correct relationship between state and nation, in which the latter is defined by language and culture' is of the greatest importance for the state's power status.[117]

Weber is aware that nation and state do not always coincide. He stresses this particular point by emphasizing that 'in ordinary language, "nation" is, first of all, not identical with the "people of a state", that is, with the membership of a given polity. Numerous polities comprise groups among whom the independence of their "nation" is emphatically asserted in the face of other groups; or, on the other hand, they comprise parts of a group whose members declare this group to be one homogeneous "nation".'[118] Weber acknowledges the existence of nations without a state and stresses the following:

Time and again we find that the concept 'nation' directs us to political power. Hence, the concept seems to refer – if it refers at all to an uniform phenomenon – to a specific kind of pathos which is linked to the idea of a powerful political community of people who share a common language or religion, or common customs, or political memories; such a state may already exist or it may be desired. The more power is emphasised, the closer appears to be the link between nation and state.[119]

The nation and power

One of the most distinguishing features of Weber's work is the emphasis he places on the significance of power within politics. In the *Freiburg Address* (1895), he relates the concept of nation to the ideal of power. He writes: 'the national state is the temporal power-organisation of the nation'.[120] A major controversy comes to light when trying to grasp to what extent Weber sustained the idea of the purely 'cultural nation'. Is it the necessary foundation of the state, as Smith and Beetham have suggested, or, as Mommsen argues, should primacy be given to the link between state and power? Mommsen stresses that 'Weber had moved far from the idea of the purely "cultural nation". He was only able to accept the national idea in association with a governmental system that pursues power politics on a grand scale.'[121] Beetham emphasizes the key role of *Kultur* in Weber's thought and remarks that: 'for Weber, *Kultur*, the promotion of what was particular to a community, was among the chief ends which alone could legitimate the exercise of state power.'[122] Albrow also stresses that 'Weber's nationalism was of a transcendent kind, that is, his commitment was to cultural ideals which the power of the state was to serve.' The point is, following Albrow's argument, that 'in a society deeply divided by class, status and religion, commitment to the "nation" just as easily could indicate detachment from particular interest groups.'[123]

However, it should be noted that Weber seems to stress the function of culture as a prime objective only after the war. Albrow confirms this point: 'throughout his later political career, in writing and activity after the Great War, Weber strove to give content to the idea that the nation was not the sum of the people's well-being, but that it was the set of values which those people were under an obligation to cherish and develop.'[124] Furthermore, Weber usually refers to economic expansion without mentioning culture: 'Our successors will not hold us responsible before history for the kind of economic organisation we hand over to them, but rather for the amount of elbow-room we conquer for them in the world and leave behind us . . . in this national state the ultimate standard of value for economic policy is "reason of state".'[125]

Weber refers to the unification of Germany as a 'point of departure for a policy of German world power'.[126] He defines power as 'the chance of a man or a number of men to realise their own will in a social action even against the resistance of others who are participating in the action'.[127] He notes that all political structures use power, but they differ in the manner in which they use it, or threaten to use it, against other political organizations. In his view, not all political structures are equally 'expansive': 'The political structure of Switzerland is "neutralised" through a collective guarantee of the Great Powers. For various reasons, Switzerland is not very strongly desired as an object for incorporation. Mutual jealousies existing among neighbouring communities of equal strength protect it from this fate.'[128]

Weber points out that Switzerland, as well as Norway, is less threatened than the Netherlands, which possesses colonies; and the Netherlands is less threatened than Belgium, which has precarious colonial possessions, and is itself at risk in case of war between its powerful neighbours. Sweden too, Weber argues, is quite exposed. In his view, the power of political structures has a specific internal dynamic. He links power with 'prestige', and notes that:

> The prestige of power means in practice the glory of power over other communities; it means the expansion of power, though not always by way of incorporation or subjection. The big political communities are the natural exponents of such pretensions to prestige.
>
> Every political structure naturally prefers to have weak rather than strong neighbours. Furthermore, as every big political community is a potential aspirant to prestige, it is also a potential threat to all its neighbours.[129]

The expansion of 'Great Power structures' is usually, but not always, determined by the economy. Weber points out that whilst trade in itself is by no means the decisive factor in political expansion, the economic structure in general does co-determine the extent and the manner of political expansion. However, he recognizes that the constant struggle of nationalities for living space and self-determination has favoured the advance of modern Western capitalism. In his opinion, the old competition between nations was intensified by the fact that the capitalist economic order, in contrast to earlier economic systems, did not necessarily favour 'physically and intellectually superior nations'.[130]

Weber regards power as a constant feature in the political arena. Power entails struggle and violence. He did not hesitate to employ the Darwinian terminology of 'the struggle for existence' and 'the survival of the fittest' to describe the inexorable character of this 'struggle of man with man for elbow room'.[131] In *Politics as a Vocation* he writes: 'the decisive means for politics is violence'.[132] Weber warns us:

> Whosoever contracts with violent means for whatever ends – and every politician does – is exposed to its specific consequences . . . I repeat, he lets himself in for the diabolic forces lurking in all violence. The great *virtuosi* of a cosmic love of humanity and goodness, whether stemming from Nazareth or Assisi or from Indian royal castles, have not operated with the political means of violence. Their kingdom was 'not of this world' . . . He who seeks the salvation of the soul, of his own and of others, should not seek it along the avenue of politics, for the quite different tasks of politics can only be solved by violence.[133]

Weber and German nationalism

The unification of Germany in 1871 strongly influenced the direction of Weber's thought. He refers to unification as a 'point of departure for a policy of German world power', and makes it clear that 'policy must not be oriented solely to supposedly objective, purely economic principles, but *it must seek the reservation and advancement of nationality as the highest principle*' (my italics).[134] Weber did not formulate a theory of nationalism but adopted a 'nationalist' attitude throughout his life. This can be illustrated by examining three particular issues: firstly, his position against Polish immigration into eastern Germany; secondly, his support of German nationalism during the First World War; and, finally, his understanding of the situation created by the Treaty of Versailles after the war.

Weber examined the agricultural situation east of the Elbe and discovered a deep and far-reaching process of transformation. The patriarchal economic order that linked the *Junker* (landlords) and the *Instmänner* (labourers), allowing the latter a relative degree of independence and security, was collapsing everywhere. This relationship had been based on a community of interests between landlord and peasants. A capitalist-oriented economy forced the East Elbian *Junker* to manage their states with capital-intensive methods, and that dissolved the ancient community of interests between the landlords and their workers. This resulted in an emigration of German labourers seeking a sure, risk-free allowance or cash salary, although this increasingly worsened their economic situation. The deciding factor was not economic but 'the powerful and purely psychological magic of "freedom" '. As a direct consequence of this, the number of Polish peasants in the area increased. Weber writes in the *Freiburg Address*: 'a lower expectation of living standards, in part physical, in part mental, which the Slav race either possesses as a gift from nature or has acquired through breeding in the course of its past history is what has helped them to expand in this zone.'[135] This development, he argues, served the economic interests of the *Junker* who were struggling with international agricultural competition. Weber deeply regretted 'from the standpoint of the state's interests' the progressive 'Polonization' of eastern Germany. He strongly recommended the closing of the eastern border to Polish immigrants and demanded a large-scale, systematic policy of internal 'Germanization' in the east: 'we do not have peace and human happiness to bequeath to our posterity, but rather the eternal struggle for the maintenance and improvement by careful cultivation of our national character.'[136]

Weber refers to the Germans as 'the more highly developed human type',[137] and urges a Germanization process along the eastern German border because 'the free play of the forces of selection does not always play out in favour of the nationality which is more highly developed or more gifted economically.' He notes that human history does not lack examples of 'the victory of less developed types of humanity and the extinction of fine flowers of intellectual and emotional life'.[138] Note the Darwinian terminology employed by Weber – 'struggle', 'fitness', 'less' and 'more highly developed types of humanity' – to refer to the relations between nations and their different stages of development, and Weber's clear German nationalist attitude.

He made no basic distinction between pure economic expansion through conquest of markets, capital exports and political imperialism. In his view, the attempt to bring the still 'free' regions of the globe under the political control of other nations was a legitimate activity from which powerful nations should benefit. Mommsen notes that 'Max Weber belonged to the circle of liberal imperialists who hoped to see the other great powers concede to Germany its fair share of the still free regions of the globe by means of a policy of increased armament.'[139]

Weber at least accepted the possibility of war and was convinced that the nation might have to make a decisive military intervention if the situation demanded it. In 1914 Weber, impressed by the national *élan* and the willingness for sacrifice with which the entire nation took up the fight for national preservation, shared the national enthusiasm and wrote: *'whatever* the outcome, *this war is great and wonderful.'*[140] Weber saw the preservation of the German Reich as a great power among the 'European world powers' as the only justifiable objective of the war. He was anxious to ensure that Germany would come out of the war with sufficient strength to fight the future battle for world position under more favourable diplomatic conditions. According to Weber, the real task of German policy in the war was not to seek territorial acquisitions of any kind beyond its national boundaries, but to create a favourable basis for a future German world policy. In 1917 he wrote: 'I would not fire one shot or agree to one penny in war loans if this war were anything but a national one.'[141]

At the end of the First World War, Weber's national feelings were aroused by the Allies' peace conditions. When he opened his lectures in Munich, he spoke with passionate national urgency: 'we can only have . . . a common goal: to turn this peace treaty into a scrap of paper.'[142] In his articles in the *Frankfurter Zeitung* he encouraged and predicted a movement of 'German irredentism' that would employ revolutionary means in order to serve national self-determination. He hoped that the Allies, alarmed by the possibility of massive 'German irredentism', would make more generous concessions to Germany: 'If the unification of all Germans (Austria!) was prevented, if Germany were forced to give up Alsace and more in the West or even (!) East-ern territories, if it were burdened with reparations to compensate Belgium, then "after an epoch of pacifism born of exhaustion, even the last worker who perceives this will become a chauvinist".'[143]

Weber's advocacy of 'irredentism' was both programme and pre-diction, and the results far surpassed all limits he could have ima-gined. Weber's nationalist feelings did not change in the course of his life. He remained a convinced nationalist, never questioning his German nationalism or submitting it to critical examination. The nation and its power in the world remained the ultimate political value for him. After the war he wrote: 'I would ally myself with any power on earth and even with the devil incarnate to restore Germany to its old splendour, if I still participated in politics. But not with the power of stupidity.'[144]

Conclusion

At this point I shall return briefly to issues raised at the beginning of this chapter. In so doing, I shall develop a comparative analysis of the writings of Treitschke, Marx, Durkheim and Weber, focusing on three points: their conception of the state, their position on German unification and their particular understanding of nationalism. Finally, I will try to answer the question of why they do not provide a systematic treatment of nationalism .

Marx's theory of the state is derived from his understanding of the history of society as the history of class struggle. Within this framework, he refers to the state as the form of organization which the bourgeoisie necessarily adopts both for internal and external purposes, and for the mutual guarantee of their property and interest. Political power is merely the organized power of one class for oppressing another. A basic transition from this point is initiated when Marx appeals to the state as independent from and superior to all social classes, as being the dominant force in society rather than the instrument of a dominant class. Marx's idea that proletarians have to conquer the political power of the state should be understood from this viewpoint.

Durkheim, by contrast, defines the state as the organ of moral discipline, social justice and social thought. The state gives dignity and rights to individuals while at the same time it imposes restrictions and limitations upon them. For him the state has a moral goal: the expansion of justice within society. Both Durkheim and Marx envisage some kind of peaceful future for humanity. Durkheim's idea that each state becomes an organ of the 'human ideal' in as much as it assumes that its main task is not to expand by extending its borders, but to increase the level of its members' morality, can be linked with Marx's goal of the abolition of the sharp economic and social inequalities derived from capitalism, establishing a world where the emancipation of all individuals as human beings would be possible. However, neither thinker gives any detailed attention to the nation-state as a generic phenomenon and neither, in a systematic way, connects the nature of the modern state with claims on territoriality and the control of the means of violence – features that will become crucial in discussing nationalism.

A radically different approach comes from Treitschke and Weber, who locate the state in the arena of constant struggle between nations. One of Treitschke's major emphases is upon power as the distinctive feature of the state. Treitschke's statements – that the state has nothing above it, has no commitments, and requires unquestioning obedience from individuals – illustrate a significant shift from Durkheim's idea that the state inevitably represents the interests of those it rules.

Two more points need to be added in order to give a complete account of Treitschke's understanding of the state: his recognition that the state is founded upon the possession of land, and the fact that the right of arms distinguishes the state from all other forms of corporate life. These two features clearly anticipate Weber's definition of the state as a 'human community that claims the monopoly of the legitimate use of physical force within a given territory'. Although Weber's theory of the state represents the most far-reaching and sophisticated of the theories analysed here – and has a great deal in it of lasting value – it does not contain a satisfactory treatment either of the nation-state or of its relation to the development of capitalism and industrialism. This is partly because Weber defines the state in such a way as to make it difficult to distinguish some of the specific characteristics of the nation-state. It is also, however, because Weber, like most theorists inclined towards the political right in these matters, tends to see violence and war as an inescapable part of the human condition.

Marx considered the nationalist objective of creating one Germany as a bourgeois claim. After 1848, however, Marx and Engels supported the national cause of the 'historic' or 'great' nations, for example Germany, in so far as large states would make it easier for the proletariat to advance its class goals.

Treitschke's and Weber's approaches to the German question again present some kind of affinity, since they both held a German nationalist attitude. Treitschke envisaged the creation of a 'Greater Germany' under Prussia's leadership. According to him, Prussia should annihilate the smaller states and incorporate them. Weber revealed his German nationalism through his opposition to Polish immigration in eastern Germany, his support of German nationalists during the First World War, and his reaction against the Treaty of Versailles. He encouraged and correctly predicted a movement of German irredentism after the First World War.

Durkheim's comments on Germany are mainly expressed in *L'Allemagne au-dessus de tout* where he explains and criticizes Treitschke's ideas as representative of the German mentality. Durkheim interprets the violation of Belgian neutrality and the Hague Convention, the systematic and inhuman war and the refusal to recognize the rights of other nationalities as deriving from Treitschke's totalitarian ideas. Durkheim refers to Germany as an example of social pathology.

On the basis of these comparisons, one can distinguish several different attitudes towards nationalism. One view regards nationalism as the most important feature of society and refers to an unquestioning acceptance of it. Treitschke and Weber stand as this view's main representatives, although it is possible to establish a certain difference between them. While in Treitschke's writings we find a definition of 'patriotism', he rarely refers to 'nationalism'; Weber has no theory of nationalism, but he does display a nationalist attitude through his statements and points of view on the historical events of his time. However, there is a main feature that unites Treitschke and Weber while at the same time distinguishing them from Durkheim and Marx: the fact that they put 'the nation' above all else. Nationality is for them the highest principle and is above all other values, including democracy itself.

A quite different attitude can be found in Durkheim's and Marx's writings since they both understood nationalism as something which needed to be transcended. Durkheim's and Marx's approaches are slightly different. Durkheim's position could be described as 'pan-nationalist'. By this I mean that his stance puts 'human' aims above 'national' ones. According to Durkheim, the 'patrie' has a key role in the process of moralization since it is the 'highest organized society that exists'. He refers to 'patriotism' as a sentiment that is about to disappear and will be replaced by what he calls 'world patriotism'.

Finally, Marx's attitude can be described as 'internationalist'. His main objective was 'universal emancipation' and he envisaged some kind of world solidarity. But he recognized that this could only be possible if nations were free from their conquerors, because only then could the workers think in international terms about a working-class solidarity.

Let us now turn directly to the issue of why there is no systematic treatment of nationalism in classical social theory. Three main reasons may be discerned for this situation. First, sociology appeared to most of the classical thinkers as closely linked to the rise of industrialization, and mainly represented an effort to gain an understanding of the new circumstances human beings had to face as a consequence of a change in the conditions and organization of labour. The Industrial Revolution completely changed the way of life of millions of people. Classical social thinkers tried to grasp the distinctive features of modern societies and focused on social changes which were the fruit of industrialization processes. The innovations taking place in the economic system produced not only a restructuring of the social bonds affecting relations between individuals in the social arena, but also a new set of ties linking individuals and political institutions, such as the state. However, nationalism was not seen as a phenomenon that could be connected to the rise of modern nation-states, or as a feature linked to the expansion of industrialism.

A second reason concerns the attempts of Marx, Durkheim and

Weber to build a 'grand theory' capable of explaining the evolution of society from its genesis to present times. In this context it becomes crucial to find a core line of argument that allows for the creation of a theory able to decode the different stages of human history.

Marx took the concept of class struggle as a central attribute of social systems, present from Ancient Greece to modern times. The centrality he conferred upon class struggle allowed him to construct a general theory of history and explain the social, political and ideological aspects of society by reference to the economy. Economic life determined social relations generally, and shaped the political sphere. In this context, nationalism was nothing other than a marginal phenomenon. I would argue that nationalism did not exist in other periods, as I consider it to be closely linked to the rise of modern nation-states. In other words, there was no sense in assuming it to be a constant feature in the different stages of human history. But nationalism as a new phenomenon was not studied or included as one of the basic traits of modern societies. Marx's emphasis upon the political sphere as 'superstructure' led him to downplay both the nation-state and nationalism as major influences upon historical change.

Durkheim saw the division of labour as a crucial characteristic in defining society. In his view, changes in the division of labour created different kinds of relations among people: organic solidarity, mechanic solidarity. The political sphere was once more left somewhat marginal. Durkheim made important contributions to the theory of the modern state, but he failed to relate the state to concepts of territoriality and violence. In his description of modern societies, he undervalued the importance of nationalism, because for him 'national aims' were secondary compared to 'human aims'.

Weber focused on rationalization as the main feature of modern societies and saw bureaucracy as an unavoidable characteristic of the rational organization of labour. It would not be accurate to say that Weber did not predict the rise of nationalism, being a nationalist himself. However, he wrote nothing about nationalism as a general feature of modern societies. Weber regarded German unification as a point of departure for a policy of 'German world power' and stressed that this policy should not be reduced to pure economic principles. Rather, it must seek the preservation and advancement of nationality as the highest principle. Weber linked his nationalism to the power and prestige of Germany. To recognize and encourage nationalism in other countries would have been against his main interest, that of German primacy. The *grandeur* of Germany became the main objective of his politics and all other values played a secondary role, being sacrificed, if necessary, in order to benefit the national principle. But despite the significance he conferred on his own nationalist attitude, rationalization was the focal point that allowed Weber to explain modern societies, shaping human relationships in the political, social and economic sphere. We have to draw upon Weber, as to some extent upon Marx and Durkheim, in discussing the nation-state and nationalism; but, again, the main thrust of Weber's thought precluded a general interpretation of these phenomena.

I would argue, therefore, that the different approaches to nationalism considered in this section are inadequate because: they ignore the dimension of nationalism as a provider of identity for individuals who live and work in modern societies; they do not develop a clear-cut distinction between nationalism and the nation-state – something which, as I shall show, it is necessary to do; they offer no theory of how nationalism can transform itself into a social movement generating political autonomy, or of its ability to homogenize individuals living in a concrete territory and sharing a concrete culture. An adequate account of nationalism needs to consider all these aspects, to connect nationalism to the idea of popular sovereignty, a notion related to the political concept of citizenship and of citizenship rights and duties, and, finally, to deal with its 'Janus-faced' character. Let me develop the implications of these points in a little more detail, to prepare the way for subsequent chapters.

(a) In my view nationalism is a sentiment that has to do with attachment to a homeland, a common language, ideals, values and traditions, and also with the identification of a group with symbols (a flag, a particular song, piece of music or design) which define it as 'different' from others. The attachment to all these signs creates an identity; and the appeal to that identity has had in the past, and still has today, the power to mobilize people.

Durkheim and Weber had both witnessed the failure of the Second International in 1914, when, in defiance of its earlier calls for 'proletarian solidarity', workers wholeheartedly joined their national armies in defence of their fatherlands against the largely proletarian armies of their enemies. In the twentieth century it appears that proletarians have perpetrated this error with such frequency that nationalist political identification would seem to be more powerful than class identification. But if this is so, it means that the sociological analysis of individuals living within modern nation-states lacks sufficient sophistication. Economic structures have often (although not by Weber) been given supreme importance in the determination of human relations, but the psycho-social need for 'identity', which I consider to be fundamental to both individuals and collectivities, has been neglected. Class identification has failed to bring people together. This is proved by two World Wars as well as the recent changes taking place in Eastern Europe, where after forty years or more of communism 'class identity' has not been able to replace 'national identities'. In Eastern Europe minorities once absorbed into sometimes 'artificially created' nation-states are now claiming independence.

(b) It is vital to insist upon the importance of a distinction between the nation-state and nationalism. I consider nationalism to be in the main a *psychological* phenomenon involving felt needs and disposi-tions, in contrast to the nation-state, which is an *institutional* one. It is also important to see that Weber, Durkheim and Treitschke understand nationalism as a phenomenon coexistent with the nation-state. In so doing, they ignore the socio-political reality exhibited in, for example, the existence of 'nationalist sentiments' in nations without a state. What happens when a nation is included, absorbed by a nation-state and becomes a nation without a state? This is a problem which exists in Western European countries such as Catalonia, the Basque Country or Northern Ireland, and it is also a phenomenon now emerging in Eastern Europe where 'old nationalities' are claiming their right to independence, their right to create independent states. Neither Durk-heim, Weber nor Treitschke considered the question: how far can a nation without a state survive or develop within an alien state? How far can a state go on recognizing and promoting other nations living within it without reaching a point of confrontation?

(c) None of the authors analysed in this section examine how a sentiment of attachment to a homeland and a common culture can be transformed into the political demand for the creation of a state. How is it possible to make this transition? What ideas lie at the base of such a dramatic change? A theory of nationalism cannot avoid this issue and, in considering it, has to deal with questions such as: how does nationalism use, and legitimate the use of, violence in its quest for the creation of a state? What is the role of nationalist ideology? Can we talk about a 'nationalist ideology' as such? What is the role of leaders in nationalist movements and how far can they contribute to the propagation of symbols and ideas?

(d) One of the most distinctive features of nationalism is its capacity to bring together people from different social levels and cultural back-grounds. In so doing nationalism shows that, however frequently nationalist feelings have been fostered and invoked ideologically by dominant elites, it is not merely an invention of the ruling classes to maintain the unconditional loyalty of the masses, making them believe that what they allegedly have in common is much more important than what in fact separates them. I do not think that millions of people around the world are so naive. Nationalist feelings are not just force-fed to an unwilling or indifferent population, although this certainly occurs. This is one of the basic factors to consider in trying to understand the persistence of nationalism.

(e) Nationalism is a phenomenon which came into being in Europe around the eighteenth century, and I shall argue that it could not have emerged without the influence of the ideas developed in the American and French revolutions. Concepts of equality, freedom, solidarity and especially popular sovereignty played a fundamental role in opening the path to nationalism. The term 'citizen' as applied to the people of a particular country served to label individuals living within specifiable political institutions. Boundaries became more and more important; the nation-state was the institution within which individuals could exercise their rights and duties and this became more evident to the subjects as the scope of the state began to penetrate their day-to-day activities.

Finally, we cannot ignore the so-called 'Janus-faced' character of nationalism. Thus, while some authors focus on the beneficial side of nationalism and closely relate it to the achievement of citizenship rights and democracy, others emphasize its noxious character by associating it with fascism in Europe and with the waging of wars. In my view, a theory of nationalism has to acknowledge its controversial character and avoid partiality. The analysis of different nationalist examples shows that it is almost impossible to present a unitary and complete pattern for all nationalisms.

In considering the way in which classical social thinkers approach nationalism, a set of questions have been raised. I am not going to develop them in this section, but I will be using them as a springboard in order to unfold their content and implications in the following chapters of this book.

2
The Political Character of Nationalism
Nationalism and the nation-state

Two major dimensions need to be considered when analysing nationalism. We must look at the ways in which nationalism both shapes and attempts to cope with the rise of the modern state; and, because the study of nationalism cannot be limited to its political character, we have to acknowledge fully the role nationalism plays as one of the major sources of identity for contemporary individuals. The idea of the nation is the most significant of several categorical identities that mediate between the autonomous but relatively weak individual and complex and powerful global forces. In a world system in which nation-states are the prime political actors, individuals are often able to transcend their finite nature through identification with the nations to which they belong. As Giner argues, the relative decline of 'supernatural' religions has contributed to the emergence of 'civil religion'. By this he means a sacralization of certain aspects of community life through public rituals, political or civil liturgies and popular devotions, designed to confer power and strengthen identity and order within heterogeneous societies. In this context, the community achieves transcendence through its symbols and epic history.[1]

This chapter develops an account of the rise of the nation-state and the ideas which led to the emergence of nationalism in Western Europe. In focusing upon the political character of nationalism, I look at the relation between nationalism and the nation-state, and emphasize the crucial role of nationalism in the modern discourse of political legitimacy. In so doing, I argue that two main types of nationalism can be distinguished: that instilled by the rulers of the nation-state as a means to homogenize its population; and that of nations without a state incorporated into larger nation-states. I consider the ways in which both types of nationalism operate; the former using the power of the nation-state, the latter developing counter-strategies to reject the 'alien state'. At the end of the chapter, I move on to consider whether nationalism can be thought of as an ideology and assess its capacity to provide a theory able to inform political action.

Definitions

In order to examine the political character of nationalism, a basic conceptual distinction between nation, state, nation-state and nationalism has to be made. By 'state', taking Weber's definition, I refer to 'a human community that (successfully) claims the *monopoly of the legitimate use of physical force* within a given territory',[2] although not all states have successfully accomplished this, and some of them have not even aspired to accomplish it. By 'nation' I refer to a human group conscious of forming a community, sharing a common culture, attached to a clearly demarcated territory, having a common past and a common project for the future and claiming the right to rule itself. Thus, the 'nation' includes five dimensions: psychological (consciousness of forming a group), cultural, territorial, political and historical. By offering this definition, I distinguish the term 'nation' from both the state and the nation-state, and I shall be using this distinction later when trying to offer an account of different forms of nationalism. By 'nationalism' I mean the sentiment of belonging to a community whose members identify with a set of symbols, beliefs and ways of life, and have the will to decide upon their common political destiny.

But there is yet another term that needs to be defined and distinguished from the ones I have just mentioned: the nation-state. The nation-state is a modern phenomenon, characterized by the formation of a kind of state which has the monopoly of what it claims to be the legitimate use of force within a demarcated territory and seeks to unite the people subjected to its rule by means of homogenization, creating a common culture, symbols, values, reviving traditions and myths of origin, and sometimes inventing them. The main differences between a nation and a nation-state, when the nation and the state do not coincide, as they hardly ever do, are that, while the members of a nation are conscious of forming a community, the nation-state seeks to create a nation and develop a sense of community stemming from it. While the nation has a common culture, values and symbols, the nation-state has as an objective the creation of a common culture, symbols and values. The members of a nation can look back to their common past; if the members of a nation-state do likewise, they may be confronted with a blank picture – because the nation-state simply did not exist in the past – or with a fragmented and diversified one, because they previously belonged to different ethno-nations. While the people who form a nation have a sense of fatherland and feel attached to a territory, the nation-state may be the result of a treaty, or the will of politicians who decide where to draw the line between states. One has only to look at the different maps of Europe that resulted from the Congress of Vienna in 1815, the Treaty of Versailles after the First World War, the modifications that followed the defeat of Hitler in 1945, and the present reshaping of Europe after the collapse of the Soviet Union.[3]

However, not all theoreticians place equal stress on the significance of the political aspect of nationalism when formulating their definitions of it. Thus, while Gellner argues that 'nationalism is primarily a political principle, which holds that the political and the national unit should be congruent',[4] Giddens points to the psychological character of nationalism, 'the affiliation of individuals to a set of symbols and beliefs emphasising commonalty among the members of a political order',[5] but undermines the political character of nationalism by remaining silent about the specific claim of nationalists in creating their own state. Kohn also advances a psychological definition of nationalism when he describes it as 'a state of mind in which the supreme loyalty of the individual is felt to be due to the nation-state'.[6] This definition is the narrowest one in so far as it associates nationalism only to the nation-state. In so doing, Kohn automatically excludes the nationalism of people lacking a state, thus ignoring one of the strongest manifestations of nationalism in our time. In my view, in understanding nationalism it is crucial to consider the will to seek and exercise state power, referring both to the claim to create a state and to the process of building it.

The origin of nations

The origin of nations is one of the most controversial issues in discussing nationalism and its political implications in particular. There are two main positions: first, the assumption that the nation is something natural. Schleiermacher talks about the nation as 'a natural division of the human race, endowed by God with its own character'. Every nationality, he proclaims, is destined through its peculiar organization and its place in the world to represent a certain side of the divine image. For it is God who directly assigns to each nationality its definite task on earth and inspires it with a definite spirit in order to glorify himself through each one in a peculiar manner.[7]

Herder, following the same line of argument, considers each nationality a manifestation of the divine and therefore something sacred which should be cultivated, not destroyed. He writes: 'for a nation is as natural as a plant, as a family, only with more branches'.[8] The sociobiological version of this argument asserts that ethnicity is an extension of kinship and that kinship is the normal vehicle for the pursuit of collective goals in the struggle for survival.[9]

The second perspective holds that the nation and nationalism are modern phenomena. Gellner correctly observes the enormous paradox that nations can be defined only in terms of the age of nationalism, rather than, as one might expect, the other way round: 'Admittedly, nationalism uses the pre-existing, historically inherited proliferation of cultures or cultural wealth, though it uses them very selectively, and it most often transforms them radically.'[10] According to Gellner, nationalism is explicable as an inevitable, or at least as a natural, corollary of some specific aspects of modernization. It is a phenomenon connected with the emergence of industrial society.[11] Giddens understands both the nation and nationalism as distinctive properties of modern states and locates the emergence of nationalism in the late eighteenth century and after.[12] Anderson also argues that nationality, 'nation-ness' and nationalism are cultural artefacts created towards the end of the eighteenth century.[13]

In my view both perspectives display inadequacies. Those based on the 'naturalness' of nations simplify the concept by including all types of human groups in the category of nations going back to the earliest periods. The theories that defend the modernity of the nation and nationalism ignore the historical roots of ethnic communities which transformed themselves into nations and later may or may not have turned into modern nation-states. In order to understand nationalism and the nation, it is worth contrasting them with pre-existing forms of group identity and loyalties. According to Barth's approach, groups tend to define themselves not by reference to their own characteristics but by exclusion, that is, by comparison to 'strangers'.[14] Thus, around the eighth century, the people who lived in what is now known as

Wales were hemmed into their territory behind a great dike and rampart raised by an alien people who called them foreigners; in the alien language they were *weallas*, Welsh.[15] It is only after a long process that we can talk about human groups which fulfil the features we have attributed to the nation, that is, consciousness of forming a community, sharing a common culture, attachment to a clearly demarcated territory, a common past and a will to decide their political destiny.

I do not consider the nation to be a purely modern phenomenon. If we look at the changes in the organization of society through time, we can see how, after the fall of the Roman and the subsequent disintegration of the Carolingian empire, Western Europe became divided into relatively small fiefs and areas of influence which by means of conquest, marriages and annexation created large units which developed a sense of community, especially by means of war against other groups. Huizinga argues that the Crusades, far from uniting in the faith those who were divided by language, descent and allegiance, reinforced the national enmities of the people of Latin Christendom by bringing them together again in martial equipment, battle array and a more or less sanctified rivalry.[16]

It was also in the period following the disintegration of Charlemagne's empire that a process of consolidation of each of the different cultures that evolved in Europe took place. Works such as *Cantar de Mío Cid* or *Chanson de Roland* were later considered as incipient examples of national cultures emerging in a soil once homogenized at an elite level by the use of Latin as the only written language. From this period onwards, although Latin continued to be the main language used by scholars, clerics and politicians, the slow but firm consolidation of national languages followed a continuous development. Thus, the framework within which national consciousness and a sense of fatherland were to evolve in Europe was established by around 1100.[17]

Smith, in trying to solve the problem of choosing between a 'natural' or a 'modern' theory of the origin of nations, develops the concept of *ethnie* or ethnic community. He analyses the nature, forms and content of its myths and symbols, its historical memories and central values, which he summarizes as the 'myth-symbol' complex. In Smith's view, 'it is *ethnie* rather than nations, ethnicity rather than nationality, and ethnicism rather than nationalism, that pervades the social and cultural life of antiquity and the early Middle Ages in Europe and the near East.'[18] But while Smith's analysis of what he calls the 'ethnic origin of nations' is illuminating in understanding the roots of the process that leads to the formation of nations, I do not consider his definition of the nation, and in particular the difference he establishes between 'ethnic' and 'territorial' nations, to be accurate. The 'territorial' nation, according to Smith, takes its basis from a sense of territory and its features include the community of laws and legal institutions, a sense of citizenship and common culture. On the other hand, he refers to the 'ethnic' nation as based on assumptions of common origins and descent, mirrored in chronicles or genealogies.[19] In my view, one has to acknowledge people's capacity for emotional attachment and identification to things external to themselves as an ever-present feature whose level and intensity are transformed through time, as are the objects of identification. Thus, kinship represents the first step in a process which was later replaced by more sophisticated forms of identification and loyalty. The Middle Ages allowed the formation of larger groups attached to a concrete territory. Through the creation of markets, the intensification of trade, the fighting of wars and the slow but progressive amplification of the state's scope, there emerged a consciousness of forming a community which differed from those of other groups outside. It is precisely at this stage that we can talk about the emergence of nations.

But, once created, these nations have possessed a common political life for different periods of time depending on particular historical circumstances, and they have pursued different political destinies since some of them were dissolved, transformed into nation-states, or divided and absorbed by other states. I consider the fact that some nations survived and created their own state as a matter of historical accident, as it is also an accident that some other nations became divided or absorbed into alien states.

Citizenship and popular sovereignty

It is usual to locate the rise of the nation-state and nationalism in late eighteenth-century Europe and to link their emergence to the ideas which gave rise to the American Revolution in 1776 and the French Revolution in 1789. I understand the rise of the nation-state as the product of a multidimensional process changing the relations of power in society. The main elements of this process included the consolidation of territorial units by bureaucratic absolutist states that for the first time were able to hold the monopoly of the means of violence inside their territory; the transformation of frontiers delimiting different states in clearly fixed borders; the emergence of the bourgeoisie as a new class especially receptive to the ideas of the Enlightenment; and the new role of monarchs and rulers which was characterized by a fundamental change in the relation between rulers and ruled. Before the eighteenth century, the right to rule was legitimated by appealing to God's will, royal blood or superior physical strength and these reasons were premised upon the belief that legitimacy came from above, rather than from the ruled. A radical shift occurred as a consequence of the spread of the new ideas of the *philosophes* emphasizing the cult of liberty, equality and particularly the idea of state power rooted in popular consent.

The concept of citizenship is closely linked to the idea of popular sovereignty. Thus, whereas the Graeco-Roman tradition of citizenship, underpinned by tradition, law and education, had required a concentration of loyalty on the city, the more complex Medieval pattern of relationships inhibited for centuries the development of a comparable civic concept, since both the Church and the Prince claimed allegiance. As Heater stresses, one of the interesting tensions in the Medieval and Early Modern eras is that between a 'regional' sense of identity and the attractions of a burgeoning nation-state. He writes, 'and yet side-by-side with this process of national integration, feelings of local or regional identity persisted to a powerful degree, sustained by memories of independent traditions and separate linguistic habits.' Only in times of national crisis would a sense of national loyalty momentarily drown out the local by its insistent call: 'The Medieval Frenchman was a *subject* of the Capetian monarch, not a *citizen* of France; likewise, the term 'citizen' was quite inappropriate to describe an Englishman's relationship with his country. In practice, the term was confined in the Middle Ages to the relationship of freely exercised rights and duties in a city or town' (my italics).[20]

In the thirteenth and fourteenth centuries, a restoration of the concept of citizenship in a political role appeared as a consequence of the renascence of Aristotle's political theory. This was soon followed by a broadening of the concept through a proliferation of studies in Roman law and history. Bartolus de Sassoferrato concluded from his study of the Roman principle of sovereignty and the concept of customary law that these Roman traditions justified the belief that the people as a whole should hold the ultimate, sovereign power and that only in a state where this held true were the people effectively free. Marsilius of Padua hesitated, however, to allow the lower orders of society a full citizen role. He held that the constitution of a state should be determined by the citizenry, and indeed that no government could be good or stable without the consent of the citizens.[21]

In the seventeenth century, Locke placed greater emphasis on the need for popular consent for the legitimacy of government. In attacking absolute monarchy he argues that the state exists to protect the lives and liberties of its citizens, so that the needs and wishes of the citizens must clearly be given high priority as an absolute right. However, the centre of the debate swiftly shifted to the question of who exactly could be considered a 'citizen', that is to say, who should be allowed the vote.

The eighteenth-century concept of popular sovereignty was designed for the 'whole people', even though in the first instance it was assumed that the most educated and enlightened citizens would have to guide the people and bring them gradually into political life. When the revolutionaries stated that the principle of sovereignty resides essentially in the nation, they may be taken to have asserted that the nation was more than the king and the aristocracy. National self-determination turned out to be one of the most frequent interpretations of popular sovereignty: 'On the principle advocated by the revolutionaries, the title of all governments then existing was put in question; since they did not derive their sovereignty from the nation, but were usurpers with whom no agreement need be binding, and to whom subjects owed no allegiance.'[22] The new principles introduced a new style of politics in which the expression of will overrode treaties and compacts, dissolved allegiance and, by mere declaration, made lawful any act.

However, the achievement of citizenship rights was by no means a process which could be taken for granted, since we can find a contrast between its defence among certain intellectual circles and the strong resistance to it on the part of the more privileged sectors of society. The attainment of citizenship rights should be viewed as a slow process launched by the French Revolution, a process that took a step backwards with Bonapartism and the 1815 Restoration, but continued to be present since the French ideals of citizenship and constitutional government provided a pattern upon which European liberals of the early nineteenth century modelled their demands. The unpleasant and degrading conditions of the proletariat brought about by the Industrial Revolution provided both the opportunity and the motive for a growth of political consciousness which expressed itself in the formation of different sorts of organizations, some of them fighting for economic and social reforms, for example trade unions. One of the more powerful reasons why demands for and concessions of reform were successful was the fear of the violent consequences of continued resistance. As Heater argues, memories of 1789 were vivid, and were in any case refreshed by 1848. The achievement of political rights, especially the right to and the possibility of direct engagement in the process of

ruling, had to be struggled for. In most European countries, enfranchisement was limited to male citizens owning a certain amount of
property – France in 1830 had a population of some 30 million while
boasting an electorate of a mere 90,000. But wealth, although it was
the main restriction on the franchise, was by no means the only one.
Religion too could disenfranchise a man, particularly if he were a
Catholic in a Protestant state, or a Jew. In Britain Catholics had to wait
until 1829 and Jews until 1858 for the right to vote.

In the United States the issue of citizenship gained complexity due
to the constitutional and legal problems of the federal–state relationship and the institution of slavery. It was not until 1865 that the
Thirteenth Amendment abolished slavery, destroying any basic distinction between black and white, and a Fifteenth Amendment was
necessary in order to confirm that: 'the right of citizens of the United
States to vote shall not be deemed or abridged by the U.S. or by any
state on account of race, colour or previous condition of servitude.'[23]
However, the struggle to achieve complete equality between individuals
of different race and colour is far from a resolution in today's world.

The universal franchise for men was mostly obtained by the early
years of the present century, while women had to wait longer. The
first groups actively organized to promote women's rights date from
the period immediately after the French Revolution. Marie Gouze, a
leader of one of the women's clubs created in Paris at that time, drew
up a statement entitled 'Declaration of the Rights of Women', based
upon the 'Declaration of the Rights of Man and Citizen', the main
constitutional document of the Revolution.[24] However, it had a less
than positive response from the male revolutionary leaders – she was
executed in 1793. In the nineteenth century feminism became more
advanced in the United States. At a meeting at Seneca Falls in 1848 a
feminist movement was launched by issuing a 'Declaration of Sentiments', consciously echoing the 'Declaration of Independence', which
proclaimed as a self-evident truth that all men and women are created
equal.[25] Despite this initiative, few real gains in improving the social
and political position of women were made during this period, until
the Nineteenth Amendment conceded female suffrage on a par with
men in 1920. The intensity of the prejudice against the involvement of
women in public affairs in the nineteenth century is crudely illustrated by the fact that when Napoleon codified French civil law, he
explicitly excluded from such legal rights minors, criminals, the men-
tally deficient and women.[26]

In Britain, Mary Wollstonecraft's *A Vindication of the Rights of Women*
(1792) stands as a predecessor of the feminism that later flourished.
When in 1866 a petition signed by 1,500 women was presented to

Parliament demanding that the electoral reforms then being discussed should include full voting rights for women, the petition was ignored. The following year, its organizers set up the National Society for Women's Suffrage. The campaign for parliamentary suffrage yielded a bitter struggle that only achieved successful results after the First World War when women were conceded voting rights because of the crucial role they had played in the war. Women in Belgium, France, Italy and Japan had to wait for the Second World War to have the same effect in their countries, while such an advanced country as Switzerland denied women participation in the federal election until 1971.

As I have tried to show above, the whole process of translating the ideas of popular sovereignty into universal adult suffrage required a long and hard struggle during which the ideas of 1789 began a slow but compelling process, and permeated to varying degrees first the educated classes and then the masses in the various European countries. Another relevant feature of the French Revolution is the emphasis it placed on education, creating as a result 'the first comprehensive system of national education to raise new generations of virtuous and patriotic citizens'.[27] Only a common education, it was felt, could realize the unity of the fatherland and the union of its citizens.

This framework made possible the rise of modern nationalism, a device which proved to be exceedingly useful for refocusing a people's loyalty away from the monarch. Monarchy by divine right was an elegantly simple device for evoking emotional attachment. But, as Heater observes, an aggregate of sovereign citizens could hardly perform that function. Then the nation, personified through symbols and rituals which symbolically recreate a sense of 'people', became the focus of a new kind of attachment. It helped to implement nationalism, the division of Europe into nation-states which favoured the definition of citizenship by nationality as well as by legal, political and social rights. Thus, as Heater argues, the French Revolution politicized the cultural concept of nationality and subsequently, during much of the nineteenth century, the association of nationalism with popular sovereignty encouraged the liberals of central and southern Europe to plot and agitate for the realization of the ideal in their own lands.[28]

The cultural nation

The primary conviction of Romantic nationalism is that culture, a particular way of life and the more important social institutions are essentially formed and shaped by the nation. They are expressions of a unitary force which is usually referred to as the soul, mind or spirit of a people; in Hegel's language, the *Volksgeist* or the character of a nation. Reflecting the uniqueness of a nation, a language is viewed as the form of expression of a particular perception of life and the world. And alongside an interest in language, there emerges a specific interest in history – the glorious past, myths of origin, customs, ways of life and ideas of a particular people: 'Romantic nationalism takes culture as its starting point, not the state, and romantic thinkers like Herder turn away from the sophisticated high culture of intellectuals and elites to the culture of the simple, pre-intellectual peoples, the *Volk*.'[29]

As Nipperdey rightly observes, Romantic nationalism could be understood as a reaction to the European intellectual hegemony based on the cultural predominance of the French-styled Enlightenment, as well as to the imperial tendencies of the Jacobins and Napoleon, illustrated by the occupation and exploitation of nations and the threat of European uniformity. But Romantic nationalism is more attuned to the conditions of stateless peoples or to outright rejection of existing states as non-national. The emphasis on linguistic-cultural identity had a different function and significance for the stateless from that which it had for those who lived in national states. For instance, Romantic nationalism had a profound effect on Catalonia. While the Napoleonic invasions had generated feelings of both Catalan and Spanish patriotism, by the 1840s Romantic historians started to glorify the Catalan past. There followed between 1833 and 1866 an intellectual attempt to revitalize Catalan culture and language known as *Renaixença*. Nevertheless, Romantic nationalism not only contributed to the creation of new nation-states, such as Germany and Italy, but also achieved prominence among the peoples of Western Europe who lived in national states, as was the case with the French.[30]

Hence, while the nationalism of the French Revolution focused on a political dimension, stressing equality among men (women were not included yet) and popular sovereignty as the only way to legitimate the power of rulers, the ideas of German Romanticism added a new character and force to nationalism in emphasizing common language, blood and soil as constitutive elements of the *Volk*.

But in studying nationalism one cannot ignore its double-edged character. Thus, while it is possible to establish tight links between nationalism, popular sovereignty, democracy and cultural originality, it would be inaccurate to neglect the use of nationalism by totalitarian regimes such as Fascism and Nazism. These regimes, by relying upon nationalist symbols emphasizing race, the 'pure archetype' of a citizen, and defending the superiority of some peoples over others, have exploited nationalist feelings, transforming them into an opposing form of nationalism defined by its exclusivist, xenophobic, expansionist and oppressive character.

So far I have described the process of modern nation-state formation and shown how it is different from both the state and the nation, although most of the theoreticians who today refer to the 'nation' clearly mean the 'nation-state'. I have located the emergence of the nation-state in late eighteenth-century Europe as the product of a multidimensional process, one that changed the relations of power in society and had as its main elements: the consolidation of territorial units by bureaucratic absolutist states, the transformation of frontiers into borders, the rise of the bourgeoisie, the new role of rulers and especially the spread of Enlightenment ideas (particularly that of 'popular sovereignty') which led to the formation of large units which only occasionally managed to unite members of the cultural nation under the rule of the state.

The nation-state and power

It is not until the nineteenth century that we find a Europe divided into clearly defined nation-states – even as late as 1871 in the case of Italy and Germany. It is precisely from this period onwards that the nation-state becomes recognized as the unit of political power *par excellence*, its form being taken as a model not only in Western Europe, but also in the rest of the world. In the twentieth century, the nation-state remains the primary actor in international relations; being a sovereign nation-state seems to be the chief international status symbol as well as to confer entrance to the world society.

As Giddens highlights, we should understand the proliferation of international institutions such as the League of Nations after the First World War as an expression of an acknowledged need for the reflexive monitoring of a worldwide system of states that furthered rather than diminished the primacy of the nation-state as the universal political form of the current era. The long-term effect of the development of supranational agents, rather than undermining the relevance of the nation-state, led it to the fore. This is because 'a state cannot become sovereign except within a system of other sovereign states, its sovereignty being acknowledged by them; in this there is a strong pressure towards mutual recognition as equals, whatever the factual situation in respect of differential power.'[31]

In the whole process of nation-state formation, state power plays a fundamental role; it is mainly by means of state power that territories become united through annexation or conquest. State power is also fundamental to a definition of the modern state through both its clear boundaries and its capacity to maintain them by the monopoly of violence. This is exerted inside the boundaries of the nation-state, but violence is also a means to defend the nation-state's interests against those of other nation-states. The power of the state upon its citizens is exerted in several ways. First, by its capacity to impose and collect taxes, which is one of the primary and more central features of the state and something that affects the day-to-day life of the citizens. Second, the state, in establishing the rights and duties of the citizens towards itself and their fellow-citizens, empowers whilst simultaneously constraining them. Third, the modern state, thanks to the development of technology, has increased and sophisticated its ability to control its citizens. The enormous expansion of the state's scope allows for the classification of citizens according to their sex, wealth, religion, age, etc., distinguishing between healthy, sick, insane, productive or unproductive people. All this leads to an increasing presence of the state in everyday life.

The modern state also has the power to control two elements that, through their role in reproducing and modifying culture, become crucial in the homogenization of the state's population: the media and education. Gellner stresses the unprecedented importance of communication and culture in industrial societies – both key features in his theory of nationalism. He writes: 'Culture is now the necessary shared medium, the life-blood or perhaps rather the minimal shared atmosphere, within which alone the members of the society can breathe and survive and produce.'[32] But culture, according to him, cannot survive without its own political shell: the state. Gellner argues: 'The state does take over quality control in this most important of industries, the manufacture of viable and usable human beings.'[33]

Finally, and keeping in mind that the nation-state receives part of its importance from the fact that we live in a world politically organized into competing nation-states, the capacity to make war is the example *par excellence* of the way in which the power of the state is exerted beyond its borders.

A decisive element of the modern state is its need to legitimate its power. As a product of the ideas about equality, liberty and popular sovereignty expanded first by liberalism and later on by doctrines like Marxism, democracy has become commonly accepted in the Occident as the 'best' form of government. There are two contrasting interpretations of modern democracy. On the one hand, the Marxist account seeks to explain the origins of democratic participation in terms of class dynamics. Capitalism and class struggle lead to the vindication of 'bourgeois freedoms' – a range of civil and political liberties – which were proposed as universal rights applying in principle to the whole of humanity. Other thinkers, like Bendix, seek to reverse the Marxist account by arguing that 'while struggles over civil and political rights were in certain historical circumstances conjoined to class conflicts, in fact the former have primacy over the latter . . . Thus the struggles that seemed to Marx to be the very prototype of class conflict in nineteenth-century Europe are seen as strivings on the part of the excluded groups to achieve full membership of the democratic polity.'[34]

Whichever of these interpretations one chooses, the development of a general awareness that political power depends upon collective capabilities has to be acknowledged as one of the main features of our time. It results in the effort on behalf of modern states to appear as the expression of the people's will. But not only governments elected by universal suffrage claim to be legitimate in the sense we have just mentioned; governments elected by more dubious means and dictatorships also claim to be the expression of the will of the people they rule.

'Legitimate' and 'illegitimate' states

Democracy implies popular sovereignty, and national self-determination may be regarded as its ultimate consequence. In this context I shall distinguish between 'legitimate' and 'illegitimate' states. By 'legitimate' state, I refer to a situation in which the state corresponds with the nation; by 'illegitimate' state, I mean a state that includes in its territory different nations or parts of other nations. This distinction is fundamental to my argument since the development of different kinds of nationalism depends upon it.

If we look at the first case – where nation and state are coextensive – we find that nationalism is favoured by the state as a means to homogenize, and increase the degree of cohesion of, its population. It is not simply that the relation of the state to its citizens is based upon a political link, but rather that the basis of this political relation is seen as an expression of the multidimensional relation which derives from the idea of forming a nation, of being a community sharing all or some of the following social elements: culture, territory, economy, language, religion and so on. The result of this is the creation of some kind of personality – 'English-ness', 'German-ness' – that emphasizes the characteristics of the citizens of a particular nation compared with those of others. In this process nationalism uses pre-existing elements of the culture of the nation, but it not only revives traditions, it also invents and transforms them. Nationalism in this kind of society where the state corresponds with the nation does not always display its colours. Rather, it permeates the day-to-day life of the nation-state and only appears at the forefront in specific situations in which the integrity of the nation-state is in danger or where there is a need to defend some interests – see, for example, the reaction of the British people to the Falklands (Malvinas) war. The appeal to nationalist reasons is also useful when a politician tries to justify his or her policy, for example: 'it's the best for our country', 'our country is not going to be left behind'.

The situation is radically different when we face what I have called the 'illegitimate' state. The inclusion of different nations or parts of nations within a state usually leads to the predominance of one nation above the others. The problem is that what would be a theoretically plausible alternative – several nations living together under the rule of a single state which evenly cares for them all – usually develops into a situation in which the state does not equally favour all the nations, or parts of nations subject to it. While all the individuals who live in the state's territory are considered 'citizens' having the same rights and duties, showing the same passport and paying the same taxes, there exists some kind of discrimination that derives from the fact that the state tries, as in the first case we have analysed here – coincidence of nation and state – to instil a common culture, a set of symbols and values and pursue a programme of homogenization among its citizens. This is so because the state, to support its legitimacy, seeks to create a nation. Furthermore, it is always easier to rule if one manages to create a sense of community among the people one governs, giving rise to the existence of links other than a mere political one.

But, if this is the case in many European nation-states, a further point could be raised in connection with the origin of many post-colonial states – or 'state-nations' – which were based upon state apparatuses originally established by the colonizing societies without any regard for the cultural units they included. Under these circumstances nationalism has usually played an important part in activating social movements stimulating the transition to independent statehood. But many problems emerge as nationalism reveals itself as a device used by elites seeking state power and proves inadequate in providing a single 'myth of origin', that is, traits and beliefs with which citizens of the state – who belong to different cultures – can identify.

When nation and state are not coextensive, there are two potential outcomes. Firstly, the state may be successful in its attempt and assimilate the different nations existing within its territory. This implies the annihilation of the cultures of the national minorities and the integration of these minorities into the main culture allowing for the formation of a coextensive nation-state.

But what happens if the state fails to assimilate the national minorities, and they perceive the state as an 'alien' institution? Under these circumstances individuals feel like 'strangers' and the state is seen as something alien to them. The 'estrangement' from the state implies a lack of identification with the policy and interests of the 'alien state'. More than this, as a 'stranger' one sees the state as a 'usurper', and thus can easily develop a strong sense of community with the members of one's minority in opposition to the homogenizing processes initiated by the state. In this situation, and in order to survive, national minorities develop counter-strategies to reject the homogenizing processes of the state. Against the nationalism inspired by the state, a nationalism of the nations 'artificially included' into the state appears. This nationalism has as its main task the rejection of the power of the 'alien state'. I would distinguish two main kinds of 'counter-strategies': cultural resistance and armed struggle. By 'cultural resistance', I mean the task of keeping alive the intellectual life of the nation, and this has different forms and levels of expression depending upon the degree of repression exerted by the state.

It is also important to emphasize the significance of the role played by the peasantry in processes of cultural resistance. The bourgeoisie in the big cities may feel tempted to adopt the 'alien state's' culture as a passport to positions of power. This took place in Spain in Franco's time when people in Barcelona spoke 'Spanish' instead of 'Catalan' because it made it easier for them to be included in the 'elite' circles of power. This situation, however, very rarely occurs among the peasantry whose social life is too localized and self-contained for them to have any interest in accepting the 'homogenizing' projects of the state; the family and the small rural community usually play a crucial role in keeping language and traditions alive.

The second counter-strategy is 'armed struggle', an attempt on the part of some nationalist groups to challenge the state's monopoly of violence. Armed struggle undermines the power of the state by showing that it is incomplete, that state officials are seen as forces of 'occupation' and that a situation of war must be acknowledged. To illustrate this, again from twentieth-century Spain, one can look at the activities of the Basque separatist movement ETA. (*Euskadi ta Alkartasuna*) in the mid-1950s and 1960s as an example of opposition to Franco's dictatorship and the strong repression exerted by the state. When armed struggle develops in a state where national minorities are strongly repressed, a sense of complicity may emerge among the members of the community. This does not mean that all the individuals of the national minority support the armed struggle or think that this is the best and only option, but very few of them would give information to the state's officials or deny their help to the members of the armed groups. It could be argued that fear of reprisals is a compelling reason, but more important is the fact that sometimes, as Pérez-Agote notes with reference to the Basque Country during the 1950s and 1960s, almost every family has one of its members or friends in prison, or is suffering the effects of brutal repression.[35] In such circumstances, the awareness of forming a community, the identification with a set of symbols and beliefs and the will to decide upon a common political destiny, increase and reinforce nationalism.

Nationalism as ideology

Nationalism as a political principle holds that the nation and the state should be congruent. If we accept democracy and popular sovereignty as the most valuable forms of government, then the self-determination of nations is just a consequence of these ideas. But does nationalism contain a doctrine able to inform political action? If a country is ruled by a 'nationalist party', does that fact give us information about the policy it will follow? Nationalist parties in nation-states and in nations without a state fulfil different needs and show distinctive characteristics. When nation and state are coextensive, the word 'nationalist' as a party label is rarely used because it is assumed that all the parties are 'nationalist' in the sense that the nation they represent already has a state of its own; 'nationalism' is taken for granted. Only on very few occasions does a party define itself as nationalist in a nation-state. This happens, for example, when a party is trying to impose a policy that implies the expansion of the nation-state (such as the National Socialist Party in Germany before 1939), or when the nation-state is threatened in one way or another and the party needs to stress its national character, perhaps in order to appeal to a certain kind of behaviour on the part of citizens (in time of war mainly, but also in peace-time: the appeal to national unity and national values serves to stimulate the sense of community of all citizens), or in Third World countries where the power apparatus is under the control of a foreign ruler – usually the colonizer, or people sponsored by it – and some parties present themselves as 'national' in order to stress their genuine character and the lack of dependence on outside agencies. Another matter concerns the use that certain politicians make of nationalist claims to justify their policies. In nation-states, it is very common to legitimate specific unpopular measures by appealing to 'the need to make a sacrifice for the nation', asserting that 'our nation deserves the effort' and so on.

In nations without a state we encounter a radically distinct phenomenon. Where the state pursues homogenization and ignores the existence of other nations within its territory, nationalist parties representing the national minorities are excluded from the polity, and are therefore often clandestine. Co-operation and solidarity between nationalist parties may lead to the defence of a unitary platform with common claims. Their first and main goal is that the state recognizes their existence and legality. In so doing, the state does not explicitly acknowledge the existence of other nations inside its territory. It can still largely ignore their demand to form a state, but, especially if it tries to present itself as democratic, it needs to show some degree of respect for the national minorities it contains. The state usually refuses to confer on them the status of 'nations', because this would undermine its integrity as a nation-state and could place its legitimacy in jeopardy. This necessitates the invention of other terms such as regions, ethnic minorities, peoples and autonomous provinces.

In the first instance, therefore, nationalism serves as a unifying factor between the parties which fight for the survival of the 'nation', and denounce their discrimination in access to goods and resources as a result of the policy of the state. But, once a certain degree of cultural and political autonomy is achieved, alliances usually disintegrate and give place to the formation of new parties. Why is this so? I shall argue that while nationalism provides a series of goals – the creation of a state, the reconstruction of the nation, the development and encouragement of the national culture and interests – it does not indicate the direction to be taken or the methods which should be adopted to achieve them. In my view, nationalism does not supply an account of the content and means of action of a party, except during a period of extreme repression and complete opposition to the state. Nationalism does not determine what politics its adherents should support. It is insufficient to know where one wants to go, one needs also to find out and decide how to get there. Thus, we can find nationalist parties following conservative, Marxist, social-democrat or liberal strategies.

Why then is nationalism so important? In my opinion, its significance lies in its capacity to represent the will of the people to be able to decide upon their own political destiny, their will to be respected as a people able to develop their culture and personality. These aspects are functions of a 'need to belong' and a sense of maintaining social and psychological integrity. Nationalism would make little sense in a world where good fellowship between cultures was possible, where powerful states felt no temptation to absorb small ones. When, rather than peaceful multiculturalism, nations feel the constant threat of being annihilated, when underdeveloped countries need to fight foreign exploitation and wage a desperate struggle to halt the starvation of their population or to explain to them why they are starving, nationalism provides a strong and useful tool to preserve culture. This is especially true for an international community of nation-states with strong tendencies to homogenization, and is one aspect of the consequences of globalization processes. The absence of nationalism in a future world can only be either the result of achieving a peaceful international community respecting and encouraging multiculturalism or the sign of a successful process of world cultural homogenization.

3
National Identity

Thus far I have presented an analysis of the political dimension of nationalism as a modern phenomenon linked to the rise of the nation-state in the eighteenth century. In what follows, I focus upon the creation of national identity and offer an account of the present day re-emergence of nationalism and its relation to a particular concern with collective, as well as individual, identity in conditions of modernity. This chapter examines three aspects. First, the development of printing and its role in the expansion and consolidation of vernacular languages. I analyse the impact of education and levels of literacy in nineteenth-century Europe and relate them to the advancement of nationalism. Second, the relationship between national identity and culture, arguing that the nation is the socio-historical context within which culture is embedded, and emphasizing the emotional investment of individuals in the elements of their culture as a key factor exploited by nationalism. I also study the role and features of identity and link them to the creation of national consciousness. Finally, in arguing that the power of nationalism stems from its capacity to create a common identity among group members, I consider the role played by symbolism and ritual in establishing and increasing nationalist feelings. My contention is that any attempt to investigate nationalism needs not only to take into account its political dimension, but also to explore less 'rational' but no less important areas concerned with feelings and emotions.

Education, literacy and national consciousness

The development of printing and the expansion of vernacular languages

By the end of the fifteenth century printing presses had been established in the larger centres of Europe, their function being the reproduction of manuscripts for the use of the Church, law, medicine and trade. At the same time, vernaculars achieved particular importance in Germany and England. In England, Gerard Groote (1340–84), the founder of the *Brotherhood of Common Life*, set up schools in which translations into the vernacular were taught as a protest against the formalism of the Church. In Germany, Luther, with the aid of the press, played a decisive role in the development of the German language. Luther 'drew on the popular speech of Middle and Lower Germany, but Thuringia and Saxony gave him his essential vocabulary . . . High German was thus established in a pre-eminent position while printing made more and more works in that language available, so that it came increasingly to seem to be the national literary language.'[1]

According to Febvre, by the seventeenth century languages in Europe had generally assumed their modern forms, and there occurred a process of unification and consolidation which established fairly large territories throughout which a single language was written. The languages which are still today the languages of each nation attained their definitive development on different time scales. The emergence of centralizing national monarchies in the sixteenth century favoured the trend towards a unified national language.[2] Printing helped to render national languages increasingly sophisticated as modes of expression. In the sixteenth century, vernaculars definitively established their claim to be languages with an independent literature. However, before the middle of the fifteenth century the ability to read and write was confined to the more successful merchants, the nobility and the clergy; indeed, primarily to the clergy, for a merchant class was slow in developing and the nobility was devoted to warfare and statecraft rather than to the gentler arts.

Wherein lies the importance of the creation of vernacular literatures and what was the role of the printing press in relation to the rise of nationalism? Anderson argues that print-languages laid the basis for national consciousness in three ways: they created unified fields of exchange and communication below Latin and above the spoken vernaculars; they gave a new fixity to language, helping to build an image of antiquity, central to the subjective idea of the nation; and they created languages of power which differed from the older administrative vernaculars.[3]

The crucial factor in this process was that, for the first time, the language in which the people of a discrete area spoke and thought was the same as that in which the ruling strata, the intellectuals and the clergy wrote and read. This was a revolutionary event, since it progressively erased the need to learn Latin if one sought to take the first step into the world of literature or science, have access to the Scriptures, or enter the realms of administration and trade. Although large numbers could not read and write, they could understand what others read in their presence. The image of someone reading, usually a story or an information-sheet, to a group of people who understood and identified the language as their own, despite the many differences between spoken vernaculars and written expressions, became a very common picture in the nineteenth century. This fact emphasized the idea of forming a community in which the members were easily identifiable through their capacity to communicate among themselves.

To be outside the limits of the nation meant, first and foremost, that one was unable to understand and be understood. The main problem of being a 'foreigner' is the inability to communicate. Lack of knowledge of the language translates into isolation and the impossibility of entering a different culture. Yet the development of vernacular languages played a decisive role in creating the image of belonging to a community. National consciousness is derived from sharing values, traditions, memories of the past and plans for the future contained within a particular culture which is thought and spoken in a particular language. I shall argue that the existence of a vernacular language is not an indispensable basis for the creation of national consciousness, although, where it exists, it facilitates that creation.

The French Revolution and education

The French Revolution did not bring about the immediate establishment of a national system of education, but it did set up the basis for its later development. One of the more important effects of revolutionary principles was that the primary control of education passed from church to state.

Education was to fulfil the needs of the newly created modern state: 'French and sciences would be emphasised . . . Civic duties and rights and loyalty to the government were to be stressed.'[4] In France, compulsory education for both sexes was introduced in 1882, at a time when there were tensions between state and church over the control of schooling, and upper and middle sectors of society hesitated about schooling the masses. In England, the elites were not prominent among those who pushed for literacy: 'Conservatives attacked charity schools, feared an educated lower class, and desired an ignorant workforce.'[5] In Spain, as late as the early twentieth century 'the church opposed the extension of public literacy and the general education of girls; it supported illiteracy on the grounds that ignorant persons could not be exposed to heretical, liberal or socialist doctrines and so would remain in a "state of grace".'[6]

But despite these tensions the growth of a reading public led inevitably to the spread of ideas that contributed to the philosophical and technological innovations that ultimately eroded the power of the clergy and the nobility, leading to new forms of political, economic, social, cultural and religious systems.

The spread of literacy in the nineteenth century

In tracing the impact of printing upon the slow decay of Latin and the emergence of vernacular languages, one should acknowledge the different levels of literacy among European countries. This factor regulated the number of people who had access to written material and therefore to the information – ideas and news – it contained.

There are striking differences among countries. Thus, whereas in France in 1854, according to parish marriage registers, 31 per cent of grooms were illiterate, in 1900 only 5 per cent were unable to sign. The decline in illiteracy was consistent and regular, usually decreasing at one percentage point per year. Rural and urban areas were affected. Women's progress was even more impressive. In 1854 46 per cent of newly-wed women were unable to sign; by 1900 only 6 per cent could not do so. Note how well their rate compared to men's literacy by the end of the century, in sharp contrast to the late eighteenth-century differential of 73 to 53 per cent literacy. Over the entire period, brides' illiteracy decreased from 73 to 6 per cent.[7] In 1854 30 per cent of the Swiss population was illiterate; England had 30 per cent male, and 45 per cent female illiteracy in 1854; Germany, only 10 to 15 per cent in 1871; and Sweden, over 90 per cent literacy in 1900. We find quite different percentages in countries like Ireland: 54 per cent illiteracy in 1841; the Austrian empire: 21 per cent of males and 25 per cent of females illiterate in 1900; not to mention the 69 per cent illiteracy in Italy in 1871. The illiteracy rate in Spain in 1877 was 63 per cent for males and 81 per cent for females. In 1931 50 per cent of Spain's adult population was still illiterate.[8]

I would argue that where we find high levels of literacy in the nineteenth century a nationalism inspired by the state was likely to develop, giving rise to the creation of more or less homogeneous nation-states. Conversely, areas with high rates of illiteracy offered the possibility of keeping alive indigenous language and culture, although these were mainly oral and only a few intellectuals who had not already been assimilated by the state's language could read and write in the vernacular. This was the case in Catalonia and the Basque Country, where, due to the poverty and lack of development of the Spanish state, minority cultures were not threatened in the same way as in France, where the state pursued a successful system of schooling leading to the decline of differences among regions and the generalization of French as the language of the country.

The role of education in 'legitimate' and 'illegitimate' states

The different levels of literacy and the expansion of schooling, as I have already mentioned, depended heavily upon the scope and power of the state. Yet as Graff rightly observes:

> The 'greatest function' of the modern school was to teach a 'new patriotism beyond the limits naturally acknowledged by its charges'. The school was first a socialising agent. The message was communicated most effectively together with reading and writing. The school's task included not only *national and patriotic* sentiments but establishing unity in a nation long divided by region, culture, language, and persisting social divisions of class and wealth. Learning to read and write involved the constant repetition of the civic national catechism, in which the child was imbued with all the duties expected of him: from defending the state, to paying taxes, working, and obeying laws. [my italics][9]

From the nineteenth century onwards, the spread of education has played a fundamental role in the configuration of national consciousnesses. The distinction between what I call a 'legitimate' state – where state and nation are coextensive – and an 'illegitimate' state – a state that includes in its territory different nations or parts of other nations – enables me to examine the different role played by education in both cases.

Where nation and state are coextensive, education and the generalization of literacy not only reinforce the possibility of communication
among people but help to develop a strong sense of community. But
there are very few examples that fit into the category of 'legitimate'
state, and very few indeed that have not at some stage managed to
absorb and assimilate cultural minorities living inside their territory.

In fact, many of the examples of present coextensivity between
nations and states are the result of successful homogenization processes. In French regions where the native tongue was other than
French the spread of literacy was retarded in the eighteenth and
nineteenth centuries. In 1789 six million people in France relied on
'foreign' languages and dialects: Flemish, Celtic, Basque, German and
thirty patois. At first, decrees were translated into the major dialects
and languages to make them more accessible to the people. But after
1792 a change in attitude occurred in an attempt to establish 'one people, one nation, one language'. As Graff mentions, with the spirit of
national linguistic development and increased intolerance of dialect,
class differences in language and literacy were reinforced. Resistance
did not prevent linguistic change. The power of the state to impose a
language and expand it through a school system was the key to initiating the slow death of minority languages and dialects. French represented the advance of civilization and progress, and its use in 'urban
and white-collar work, armed-forces training, and the growing volume
of print materials stimulated the increase in French speaking, reading
and writing in the countryside'.[10]

Among other attempts at homogenization with different outcomes
from that of France, we can refer to nineteenth-century Prussia, where
Bismarck expanded the Prussian school system into the Polish regions
of Poznan and Silesia and allowed only the German language as a
medium of instruction. At the same time the Russians were pursuing a similar policy, centred on the Orthodox Church, and had even
embarked on a campaign to eliminate the Polish language and culture
by actively impeding the Catholic Church, banning private schools
and establishing Russian state schools. In 1869 the Hungarians promoted a policy of compulsory Magyarization; the ability to read and
write Magyar being made a precondition for enfranchisement.[11]

When the state manages to impose a culture and a language, and,
through this, develop a sentiment of patriotism among its citizens, as
was the case in France, we can affirm with Gellner that 'it is nationalism which engenders nations.'[12] The state favours nationalism as
a means to increase the links existing among its citizens. If the state
is successful and, apart from the mere political connection, manages
to develop a combination of several kinds of relations – economic,

territorial, religious, linguistic, cultural – the state creates the nation. But we confront a radically different situation when homogenization is only partially or not at all achieved. The nationalism of minorities resisting assimilation, I would argue, presents fundamental differences in origin and purpose compared with the nationalism instilled by the state in order to create the nation, and does not correspond to Gellner's definition. This nationalism is often defined as 'peripheral nationalism' for it emerges not from the state, but rather from nations or parts of nations included in a large state.

The educational demands of the nineteenth century, accentuated by the impact of Romanticism, proved to be significant factors in the advent of nationalisms in nations without a state. It is possible for minorities to maintain their language and culture, even though they have no state to protect them, if they are living in a world characterized by oral traditions. But when, as was progressively the case in the nineteenth century, the state's scope increases and imposes language and culture by means of a well-organized system of education, the existence of minorities is threatened. As a result, in Europe some nations were assimilated into large nation-states, whilst others developed powerful nationalisms that in some cases led to the formation of new states, as was the case after the Treaty of Versailles in 1919. But again, when in 1919 and after 1945 there was a redrawing of the map of Europe, the various new nation-states regarded education as the key to national and cultural identity.

Now, as a result of the disintegration of the USSR, we are witnessing a re-emergence of nationalism, especially in Eastern Europe.[13] Each time nationalism comes to the fore, there is a great interest in controlling education, publishing and the use of vernaculars, and in emphasizing the traits and symbols specific to every particular *Volk*. Once more nationalism uses and needs the power of the press and the control of education to reach the masses. Levels of literacy have risen impressively all over Europe and this means that the number of potential readers and writers has grown enormously. In addition, a revolution affecting the media has resulted in the creation of a wide range of intercommunication tools, characterized by their accuracy, their fixity and especially by their instantaneousness. The nationalisms of the twentieth century are able to take advantage of these new devices and use them to diffuse their messages. Changes affecting the media are playing a crucial role in the development of current nationalisms. I shall return to this shortly, since I draw upon it in my own discussion of the interconnection between the local and the global, and the effects of globalization processes upon the present unfolding of nationalism.

National identity and culture

Identity

In the first chapter I argued that there is no systematic treatment of nationalism in the work of Treitschke, Marx, Durkheim and Weber. Their different approaches to nationalism are partial and inadequate because they ignore the dimension of nationalism as a creator of identity for individuals who live and work in modern societies. With this in mind, I shall look at the way in which identity is formed and its relation to nationalism.

Baumeister argues that medieval European attitudes lacked the modern emphasis on individuality since society operated on the basis of lineage, gender, social status and other attributes, all of which were fixed by birth. He points out that 'only with the emergence of modern societies, and in particular, with the differentiation of the division of labour, did the separate individual become a focus of attention.'[14] By the late Middle Ages, people increasingly learned to think in individual terms and slowly solidified concepts of the single human life as an individual totality. Baumeister's analysis recalls that of Durkheim: 'the "individual", in a certain sense, did not exist in traditional cultures, and individuality was not prized.'[15]

Thus, while the eighteenth century's rejection of the Christian models of human potentiality and fulfilment led the Romantics into a passionate search for new, secular substitutes, the rejection of the legitimacy of the traditional, stable political and social order led to a troubled recognition of the pervasive conflict between the individual and society. Yet, in the nineteenth century, the prestige of the individual self reached an all-time high that declined in the early twentieth century when 'new social arrangements and events dramatized the relative powerlessness of the individual leading to a devaluation of the self.'[16] However, a process giving special significance to the 'uniqueness' of each individual led to a particular concern about identity reflecting the individual and collective (group) desire to be 'different'.

The key question with regard to identity is 'Who am I?' Identity is a definition, an interpretation of the self that establishes what and where the person is in both social and psychological terms. When one has identity one is situated; that is, 'cast in the shape of a social object by the acknowledgement of [one's] participation or membership in social relations'.[17] Identities exist only in societies, which define and organize them. As Baumeister puts it: 'the search for identity includes the question of what is the proper relationship of the individual to society as a whole.'[18] This search is also evident at the individual level through the need to belong to a community. In the current era the nation represents one of these communities: national identity is its product.

The defining criteria of identity are: continuity over time, and differentiation from others,[19] both fundamental elements of national identity. Continuity springs from the conception of the nation as a historically rooted entity that projects into the future. Individuals perceive this continuity through a set of experiences that spread out across time and are united by a common meaning, something that only 'insiders' can grasp. Differentiation stems from the consciousness of forming a community with a shared culture, attached to a concrete territory, both elements leading to the distinction between members and 'strangers', 'the rest' and 'the different'.

Identity fulfils three major functions: it helps to make choices, makes possible relationships with others, and gives strength and resilience.[20] First, to be fully expressed and developed national identity requires that the people forming the nation enjoy the right to decide upon their common political destiny. Second, if we consider it at a personal level, national identity obviously makes relationships with others possible, since the nation appears as a common pool where individuals with a common culture live and work creating a world of meaning. But, above and beyond this, the claim of nations to have a state is the claim to be recognized as 'actors' within the global system of nation-states. Finally, national identity gives strength and resilience to individuals in so far as it reflects their own identification with an entity – the nation – that transcends them. Also, nationalist ideologies usually encourage the development of the nation and present it as worthwhile. Although on some occasions they focus upon past splendours, they always promise a better future and advocate regeneration.

But how does the individual experience his or her national identity? I suggest that community of culture and unity of meaning are the main sources that allow the construction and experience of national identity. As a collective sentiment, national identity needs to be upheld and reaffirmed at regular intervals. Ritual plays a crucial role here. As Durkheim argues in *The Elementary Forms of the Religious Life*, there is little difference between religious and civil ceremonies in their object, the results which they produce, or the processes employed to attain these results. Durkheim emphasizes the power of ritual, a theme I have already discussed in Chapter One, and what he writes about religion can easily be applied to national ceremonies:

> Truly religious beliefs are always common to a specific group which
> professes to adhere to them and to practise the rites connected with
> them. They are not merely received individually by all members of the
> group; they are what gives the group its unity. The individuals who
> compose the group feel themselves bound to each other by the very fact
> that they have a common faith.[21]

Individuals, through their identification with the nation, can be compared with believers. To paraphrase Durkheim, the believers who have
communicated with their god are not merely people who see new
truths of which the unbeliever is ignorant; they are individuals who
are stronger, feel more powerful in enduring the trials of existence or
in conquering them: 'It is as though they were raised above the miseries
of the world, because they are raised above their condition as mere
men.'[22] I shall return to these issues when considering the symbolic
content of nationalism.

Melucci defines collective identity as 'an interactive and shared
definition produced by several interacting individuals who are concerned with the orientations of their actions as well as the field of
opportunities and constraints in which their action takes place'.[23]
Collective identity considered as a process involves: formulating cognitive frameworks concerning the goals, means and environment of
action; activating relationships among the actors, who communicate,
negotiate and make decisions; and making emotional investments,
which enable individuals to recognize themselves in each other.

I understand the present revival of nationalism as a response to a
need for collective as well as individual identity. Parsons suggests the
term 'de-differentiation' to explain the need for collective identity
among particular groups. He argues that:

> There is a growing plurality of social roles in which the individual is
> called upon to act. Yet none of these roles is able adequately to offer the
> individual a stable identity. Selective mechanisms of de-differentiation
> thus come into being to provide identity via a return to primary mem-
> berships. Thus ethnicity is revived as a source of identity because it
> responds to a collective need which assumes a particular importance in
> complex societies.[24]

As Melucci points out, national movements bring to light two problems central to more structurally complex societies: they raise questions about the need for new rights for all members of the community,
particularly the right to be different; and they claim the right to autonomy, to control a specific living space (which in this case is also a

geographic territory).[25] In terms of political action this means fighting for new channels of representation, access for excluded interests to the political system, and the reform of decision-making processes and the rules of the political game.

The current re-emergence of nationalism not only responds to the gulf between political and cultural processes, but also gains strength as other criteria of group membership (such as class) weaken or recede. National solidarity also responds to a need for identity of an eminently symbolic nature in so far as it provides roots based on culture and a common past and offers a project for the future. As Melucci writes:

> The 'innovative' components of ethno-national movements, albeit a minority issue bound up with their struggle against discrimination and for political rights, also has a predominantly cultural character. The ethnic appeal launches its challenge to complex societies on such fundamental questions as the goals of change and the production of identity and meaning . . . Difference is thereby given a voice which speaks of problems which transverse the whole of society.[26]

Culture

How is identity created? One of the main features of humans is their ability to adapt to different environments. The individual is flexible and contains many possibilities for his or her later development. The biological basis of humans allows their extraordinary capacity for social learning and thus the richness and variety individuals are able to display through the development of a wide range of diverse cultures. Individuals with all their potential are socialized and raised within a group that is located in space and time. Values, beliefs, customs, conventions, habits and practices are transmitted to the new members who receive the culture of a particular society. The process of identification with the elements of a specific culture implies a strong emotional investment. All cultures single out certain parts of a neutral reality and charge them with meaning. Individuals are born within cultures that determine the way in which they view and organize themselves in relation to others and to nature.

Two major implications deriving from this possess a particular significance for the analysis of nationalism. First, a common culture favours the creation of solidarity bonds among the members of a given community and allows them to imagine the community they belong to as separate and distinct from others. Solidarity is then based upon the consciousness of forming a group, outsiders being considered as strangers and potential 'enemies'. Second, individuals who enter a culture emotionally charge certain symbols, values, beliefs and customs by internalizing them and conceiving them as part of themselves. The emotional charge that individuals invest in their land, language, symbols and beliefs while building up their identity, facilitates the spread of nationalism. Thus while other forms of ideology such as Marxism or liberalism require the indoctrination of their followers, nationalism emanates from this basic emotional attachment to one's land and culture. Social and political theory has tended to place emotions and feelings outside the sphere of its enquiry, considering the irrational inevitably inferior to the rational. My point is that the force of nationalism springs not from rational thought alone, but from the irrational power of emotions that stem from the feelings of belonging to a particular group. The double face of nationalism results from the way in which these emotions are either transformed into a peaceful and democratic movement seeking the recognition and development of one's nation, or turned into xenophobia, the will to put one's nation above others and eradicate the different.

From a symbolic perspective, 'culture is the pattern of meanings embodied in symbolic forms, including actions, utterances and meaningful objects of various kinds, by virtue of which individuals communicate with one another and share their experiences, conceptions and beliefs.'[27] A common culture, as I have already stressed, has the ability to create a sentiment of solidarity that derives from the consciousness of forming a group. A common historical past which includes 'having suffered, enjoyed, and hoped together',[28] and a future common project, reinforce the links among the members of a given community. As symbolic forms, cultural phenomena are meaningful for those who take part in them and the meaning is something that only 'insiders' know and value.

On Gellner's theory of nationalism

Gellner's writings probably supply the best starting-point for a discussion of the role of culture in the creation of nationalism. Gellner's main emphasis is upon the distinctive character of nationalism as 'rooted in a *certain kind* of division of labour, one which is complex and persistently, cumulatively changing'.[29] According to him, industrial society is based upon perpetual economic growth; the need to fulfil economic necessities engenders mobility which at the same time produces egalitarianism. Industrialism involves a complex division of labour and this requires a rather different, specialized and universal educational system which provides people with the basic tools for employment, which are a standard language and literacy. To sustain an educational system whose function is the production of a 'standard culture', one needs a centralized state. Gellner points out that the state is charged with the maintenance and supervision of an enormous social infrastructure, and that universal literacy is required of industrial society. However, I would argue that in the early stages of industrialism, which correspond to the first expressions of modern nationalism found in the late eighteenth century, literacy was only important among managers and clerks. Thus, Gellner's description of the role of the state in education only reflects the situation achieved in the mid-twentieth century, though it claims to apply to earlier industrial societies, specifically to late nineteenth-century Europe.[30]

On the other hand, one can accept that a mass education system is a universal product of industrial societies, but, as Breuilly remarks, 'does the answer lie in the generic training such education offers?'[31] Gellner's explanation sounds quite functionalist: education may eventually operate as he envisages, but does that explain its development? Unless one specifies either a deliberate intention on the part of key groups to produce this result, or some feedback mechanism which will 'select' generic training patterns of education against other patterns, this cannot count as an explanation. Besides, it is possible to think of other reasons: the need to train citizens or conscripts for the mass politics and mass armies of the modern age, humanitarianism, or the need to occupy children's time as soon as they began to be excluded from the labour force.

Gellner's assumptions about industrialism can also be subjected to criticism. Yet he pays little attention to the mechanics of state-formation and deliberately turns his attention from capitalism to industrialism. One might respond by saying that nationalism exists and has existed in numerous non-industrial states. At the same time, all nationalisms claim to be historically rooted in traditions formed long before the industrial era. It seems to me that Gellner's description is useful for developing an understanding of events in Western Europe, while having less value in interpreting, for example, the Chinese experience.

Two fundamental questions still need to be posed. The first concerns the power of nationalism; the second refers to the capacity of nationalism to bind together people from very different cultural levels and social backgrounds. Liberalism and Marxism, two of the most important systems of thought from which social scientists draw, both predicted the decline of national feelings. Liberalism expected the decline of nationalism because 'trade flows across frontiers; the life of the intellect ignores frontiers; and with the progress of learning, wealth and industry, the prejudices and superstitions and fears which engender frontiers would decline.'[32] For a Marxist it appears inexplicable because only abysmal cognitive error could lead the proletariat to identify with the exploitative ruling classes of the society to which they belong against the exploited masses (and ruling classes) of another society.

Gellner, however, attempts to demonstrate that nationalism can best be understood as a necessary consequence of the very forces described by liberals and Marxists. He does so by showing how industrialism's demands for homogeneity lead to the creation of culturally unalloyed nations. To explain nationalism as a consequence of a high division of labour and a common culture seems to me an extremely simple conception when applied to a world in which globalization processes favour constant cultural interconnections. If Gellner is right, we should be witnessing a tendency towards a single uniform world nationalism. But in fact the effect is exactly the opposite. Old nationalisms are recovering strength and very few people wish to give up their original national identity, despite belonging to backward nations, in order to adopt a more 'successful' one. When Gellner writes, referring to individuals living in industrial societies, 'for most of these men, however, the limits of their culture are the limits, not perhaps of the world, but of their own employability and hence dignity'[33], he does not take into consideration that, whenever a nation is oppressed, a considerable number of individuals will sustain their dignity as members of a particular culture even at the cost of seeing their chances of getting a job substantially undermined and, in some extreme cases, even facing exclusion from the labour market.[34]

Furthermore, while Gellner emphasizes how 'ardently' national identification may be felt, he does not provide a satisfactory account of how the functional imperatives he invokes can generate such powerful feelings. Seton-Watson set out to understand 'this force of nationalism which has continued to shake the world in which we have lived'.[35] Carr refers to 'the dynamite of nationalism'.[36] Dunn writes: 'no one could doubt that it has become one of the more ebullient and energising principles.'[37] But does Gellner's theory confer upon nationalism sufficient intellectual strength to sustain such a role? I think not. Gellner does not explain the willingness of modern populations to die in their thousands for their country (and its often repulsive rulers).

Contrary to Gellner, I argue that the power of culture lies in its capacity to create identity, something that individuals cannot live without and that cannot easily be changed. Culture cannot be reduced to the entrance card for a concrete labour market. Culture designs the most intimate parts of humans, mediating the way in which they relate to themselves, others and the exterior world. A common culture presumes some kind of complicity that only individuals socialized within that culture can understand. Individuals do not enter a foreign culture merely by learning the language of that culture. They have the necessary tools, but it takes a long time before they are able to capture the meaning implicit in words, expressions and rituals. This 'complicity' contributes to the creation of a common consciousness and the development of links of solidarity among group members.

The attachment of individuals to their community is a constant that has adopted diverse forms through different historical periods. Loyalty has focused upon various entities: the clan, the tribe, the city, the dominion of a particular lord, the monarch and, from the eighteenth century onwards, the nation. When Gellner argues that: 'Modern man is not loyal to a monarch or a land or a faith, whatever he may say, but to a culture',[38] he fails to contemplate the role of culture in the creation of identity. This, I argue, is the main explanation for the 'loyalty' of individuals to this abstract entity that transcends their lifespan. In my view, the nation, personified through symbols and rituals which symbolically recreate a sense of 'people', has become the focus of a new kind of attachment. The nation represents the socio-historical context within which culture is embedded and by means of which culture is produced, transmitted and received.

Gellner is right in suggesting that: 'The state is, above all, the protector, not of a faith, but of a culture, and the maintainer of the inescapably homogeneous and standardising educational system.'[39] However, he ignores a further dimension of this issue by failing to distinguish between what I call the 'legitimate' and the 'illegitimate' state. In the former, where nation and state are coextensive, Gellner's definition works perfectly. But in the second situation, where several nations or parts of nations are bound together under the rule of a single state, the state must decide which culture is to be given priority and how to implement a successful policy of cultural homogenization. This raises doubts about the viability of a state that compromises itself with the protection and encouragement of different cultures evolving within it. For instance, this would be the case in Spain where, as a result of the 1978 Constitution, Catalans and Basques, among other national minorities included in Spain, now see their cultures recognized and protected. How far can a state go in acknowledging and encouraging (financing) different cultures within its territory without threatening the cultural homogeneity that Gellner considers necessary if industrial societies wish to prosper? By neglecting this point, Gellner fails to tackle one of the major problems faced by contemporary European societies where political units are mainly characterized by the non-coextensivity of nation and state. To solve this question by means other than the use of force, a detailed and careful analysis of these issues is required, especially since the threat of further fragmentation is increased by the present influx of immigrants from Eastern Europe, Asia and Africa into Western Europe.

Within a given community a hierarchical division among its members may be seen as a constant factor promoting social tension, social unrest and social change. However, when the integrity of the group is in danger, the solidarity that comes from shared values, beliefs and ways of life proves that the proletarian of a particular nation feels that he or she has more in common with the exploitative ruling classes of the society he or she belongs to than with the exploited masses – and ruling classes – of another society. Dunn states that, 'certainly socialism has never looked the same since the parties of Engels and of Jaurès slunk into line and agreed to defend their fatherlands against the aggression of the largely proletarian armies of their foes.'[40] This same strong sentiment of solidarity is what makes people ready to die for their nation in their thousands. Preservation of the self and the group to which one belongs is the primary concern in time of crisis. Additional weight is added to this by the fact that our global political system is organized into nation-states, these being the only actors recognized at an international level.

The symbolic content of nationalism

On symbols

Symbols and rituals are decisive factors in the creation of national identity. The nation as a form of community implies both similarity among its members and difference from outsiders. As Anthony Cohen puts it, a boundary marks the beginning and end of a community in so far as it encapsulates its identity.[41] Boundaries are called into being by the exigencies of social interaction. However, not all boundaries and not all components of any boundary are so objectively apparent. They may be thought of, rather, as existing in the minds of their beholders. Boundaries are symbolic in character and imply different meanings for different people. Yet, if we consider the boundary as the community's public face, it appears as symbolically simple, but as the object of internal discourse it is symbolically complex. 'The boundary', Cohen argues, 'symbolises the community to its members in two different ways: it is the sense they have of its perception by people on the other side – the public face and "typical" mode – and it is their sense of the community as refracted through all the complexities of their lives and experiences – the private face and idiosyncratic mode.'[42]

The consciousness of forming a community is created through the use of symbols and the repetition of rituals that give strength to the individual members of the nation. By favouring occasions in which they can feel united and by displaying emblems – symbols – that represent its unity, the nation establishes the boundaries that distinguish it from others. A symbol was originally an object, a sign or a word used for mutual recognition and with an understood meaning that could only be grasped by the initiated. The meaning of a symbol cannot be deduced. Symbols only have value for those who recognize them. Thus they provide a revealing device to distinguish between members and 'outsiders' and heighten people's awareness of, and sensitivity to, their community. The soldier who dies for his flag does so because he identifies the flag with his country. By means of this association he loses sight of the fact that the flag is merely a sign. As a symbol the flag is valuable: it represents the country.

All communities use symbols as markers. Symbols not only stand for or represent something else, they also allow those who employ them to supply part of their meaning. Hence if we consider a flag as a symbol of a particular country, its meaning cannot be restricted to the relationship flag–country. Rather, it achieves a special significance for every individual since the flag – as symbol – has the power to evoke particular memories or feelings. Symbols do not represent 'other things' unambiguously. They express 'other things' in ways which allow their common form to be retained and shared among the members of a group, whilst not imposing upon them the constraints of uniform meanings. An example of the malleability of nationalist symbols is that people of radically opposed views can find their own meanings in what nevertheless remain common symbols. The *senyera* – the Catalan flag – for instance, although representing a country, Catalonia, holds different meanings for socialist, nationalist, republican or right-wing Catalan parties, which use it in their demonstrations and other public events.

It is important to emphasize that symbols are effective because they are imprecise. They are, as Cohen states, 'ideal media through which people can speak of a "common" language, behave in apparently similar ways, participate in the "same" rituals . . . without subordinating themselves to a tyranny of orthodoxy. Individuality and commonalty are thus reconcilable.'[43] I shall argue that the nation, by using a particular set of symbols, masks the differentiation within itself, transforming the reality of difference into the appearance of similarity, thus allowing people to invest the 'community' with ideological integrity. This, in my view, explains the ability of nationalism to bind together people from different cultural levels and social backgrounds. Symbols mask the difference and highlight commonalty, creating a sense of group. People construct the community in a symbolic way and transform it as a referent of their identity.

According to von Bertalanffy, symbols are signs that are freely created, represent some content, and are transmitted by tradition.[44] However, although part of the strength of symbols stems from their capacity to express continuity with the past, they need to be constantly reinterpreted, and even re-created, in order to avoid the danger of becoming stereotyped, decorative or meaningless. Symbols possess an inherent non-static character, they are subject to an evolution that, as Sperber mentions, can take place not only from generation to generation, but also within one generation because the period of acquisition of symbolism is not limited to a particular chronological age.[45]

If the symbols that represent the nation receive a completely fixed, restricted and confined interpretation, they will probably die and become 'empty shells of fragmentary memories'.[46] Nationalism, to retain the vitality of its symbols, must constantly readapt and reinterpret them within fresh contexts. Symbols have their origin in the past, but the power of nationalism lies not only in expressing this fact and linking symbols with tradition; rather, nationalism has also both to re-create old symbols and create new ones to maintain and increase the cohesion of the nation.

As Durkheim argues, societies are likely to create 'gods' during periods of general enthusiasm, and he mentions the French Revolution as a period in which 'things purely laical by nature were transformed by public opinion into sacred things: these were the Fatherland, Liberty, Reason. A religion tended to become established which had its dogmas, symbols, altars and feasts.'[47] However, it would be a mistake to think that elements once elevated to the category of symbols can remain as such forever. The celebration of the bicentennial of the French Revolution in Paris was an example of the evolution of symbols once adopted to represent the nation. Symbols have become transmuted to fulfil the task of increasing a sense of community in a radically different society from that of 1789.

On rituals

Symbols are usually used as key elements in common rituals that hold together the members of the nation at regular intervals. In analyzing the way in which national symbolism and ritual operate, Durkheim's study of religion is particularly relevant.

Nationalism began to gain strength when religion was declining in Europe, and, in my view, Durkheim was fundamentally right in arguing that 'it is, indeed, a universal fact that, when a conviction of any strength is held by the same community of men, it inevitably takes on a religious character.'[48] Nationalism as religion has its rites, and these are not merely received individually. Rather, as Durkheim stresses, they are what give the group its unity: 'The individuals who compose the group feel themselves bound to each other by the very fact that they have a common faith.'[49] A common faith requires a 'church', and it could be argued that the 'nation' fulfils this role, while intellectuals could be equated with priests. As beings sharing the same totemic principle, the members of the same nation feel morally bound to one another. But, as members of the tribe, the individuals who form the nation need to renew and give strength to the community they form by periodically reviving their ideals.

Individuals who share the same culture, feel attached to a concrete land, have the experience of a common past and a project for the future, need to create occasions in which all that unites them is emphasized. In these moments, the individual forgets about himself or herself, and the *sentiment of belonging* to the group occupies the prime position. The collective life of the community stands above that of the individual. Through symbolism and ritual, individuals are able to feel an emotion of unusual intensity that springs from their identification with an entity – the nation – which transcends them, and of which they actively feel a part. On these occasions the members of the nation receive strength and resilience, and are able to engage in heroic as well as barbaric actions in order to protect the interest of their nation. As Durkheim points out, 'because he is in moral unison with his fellow men, he has more confidence, courage and boldness in action, just like the believer who thinks that he feels the regard of his god turned graciously towards him.'[50]

The creation of national identity, I argue, responds to a complex process by which individuals identify themselves with symbols that have the power to unite and stress the sense of community. This process of identification involves a continuous flow between individuals and symbols, in the sense that individuals do not merely have to accept already established symbols, but rather have constantly to re-create them and attribute to them new meaning according to the changing circumstances through which the life of the community develops. Tradition has to be reinvented and persistently actualized. Yet if, as Renan argues, the nation is the result of a daily plebiscite, the identification with its symbols also needs to be worked out constantly to avoid the risk of losing meaning. If this happens, the sense of community immediately weakens. All groups need symbols and rituals in order to survive, maintain cohesion and reaffirm the collective ideas which they create. Durkheim acknowledged this when he wrote: 'It is by uttering the same cry, pronouncing the same word, or performing the same gesture in regard to some object that they [individuals] become and feel themselves to be in unison.'[51]

4
Nationalism, Racism and Fascism

The controversial character of nationalism derives from its weakness as an ideology capable of informing political action. The nationalist discourse is employed by minorities seeking self-determination and nations willing to develop their own cultures while respecting the identical rights of their neighbouring groups. But nationalism is also used in association with various forms of discrimination that imply a categorization of individuals depending upon their national identity. In this context, nationalism may be invoked by those displaying racist, xenophobic and fascist attitudes and frequently involves the use of several forms of violence.

This chapter aims to explore the elements of racist and fascist discourses and their relation to nationalism.

Race

Race is a way of naming the difference between members of a particular collectivity and the 'other', 'the alien'. Race establishes a boundary between those who share certain biological or physiognomic characteristics which 'may or may not be seen to be expressed mainly in culture or life-style but are always grounded on the separation of human populations by some notion of stock or collective heredity of traits'.[1] Race as a concept has its origins in the nineteenth century. Its primary use was and still is the classification of individuals on the assumption that differences in the phenotype are synonymous with variations in intellect and abilities.

The idea of 'race' derives from a period of colonial expansion and was widely employed as a legitimizing argument for European domination. As Golberg points out, race 'in articulating as natural ways of being in the world and the institutional structures in and through which such ways of being are expressed both establishes and rationalises the order of difference as a law of nature'.[2]

In terms of the Darwinian revolution, race signifies a subspecies, breeding population or common gene pool. Gobineau conflates race with basic linguistic groups. He argues that each race has its own natural language proper to it. In the nineteenth century, European linguists looked to affinities and differences in the system of linguistic representation of the various language groups rather than to physical traits when classifying races. The prevailing meaning of race at any intersection of time and place is, as Golberg shows, embedded in and influenced by the pre-eminent conditions within the social milieu in question.[3] At first race became identified with class or status, later it meant culture, ethnicity or nation.

However, there are substantial arguments that question the scientific validity of the concept of race. It is highly problematic to decide scientifically who belongs to a particular race, given the constant mixing of the gene pool. Furthermore, the idea of social and intellectual excellence or backwardness depending on 'race' is clearly unsustainable.[4]

Two key ideas should be taken into account when thinking about race. First, 'race' is an arbitrary, historically changing concept. Second, although the scientific validity of 'race' is questionable, classification according to physical differences maintains an indisputable strength which derives from the visibility of physical traits. A further point concerns the eminently social character of race as a cornerstone in the construction of social relations within given societies. The concept of 'race' cuts across nation-state boundaries; however, discrimination, classification and the organization of social relations between 'races' takes place within nation-states that have the power to enforce particular policies containing ways to include and exclude individuals, allocate power and resources to selected groups and decide who is and who is not entitled to become a citizen.

Racism

Racism is an ideological discourse based upon the exclusion of particular collectivities because of their biological or cultural make-up. The specificity of racism lies in its constant invocation of a difference that attributes superiority to one group to the detriment of another, and favours the growth of hostile feelings towards those who have been defined as 'different'. Racism involves a negative evaluation of the other that requires an active censorship of any tendency to regard him or her as an equal. This process generates the emergence of boundaries that 'change over time in response to concrete economic, political or ideological conditions'.[5] Cultural preservation, fear of the unknown and, above all, the maintenance of a political–economic *status quo* are among the reasons given by those subscribing to racism. The use of stereotypes contributes to what is presented as a clear-cut distinction between individuals who are classified and attributed a set of positive or negative characteristics depending on their race.

The key role of racism since its early manifestations in colonial times has been the denial of social, political and economic participation to certain collectivities and the legitimation of various forms of exploitation. Racism is embedded in power relations. It reflects the capacity of a certain group to formulate an ideology that not only legitimizes a particular power relation between ethnic communities but represents a useful mechanism for the reproduction of such relation. Cashmore and Troyna define racism in a modern sense as the combination of prejudice plus power. In their view prejudice reflects an 'inflexible mental attitude towards specific groups based on unreliable, possibly distorted stereotyped images of them'.[6]

When considering racist attitudes, power fulfils a fundamental role in three different ways. First, power within the racist discourse is epistemologically exercised in the dual practices of naming and evaluating the other.[7] Both activities permit the classification of individuals and attribute a passive role to them. They receive what the holder decides.

Second, the socio-political consequences of racism are subjected to the power possessed by the racists. Thus a group may consider their neighbours as endemically inferior, but if they do not possess power to implement their racist views, these would be limited and have no transcendence. What made possible the holocaust was the combination of a racist discourse with the political, social and economic power to make it effective.

Third, when a group imposes a world-view that contains racist elements, the society in question becomes automatically divided between minority and majority groups. Minority groups, Spoonley argues, 'are not necessarily numerically smaller but are those groups who face prejudice and unequal treatment because they are seen as being inferior in some way'.[8] In this context 'minority' reflects relative lack of power. A 'majority group', by contrast, possesses political, economic and ideological power. The 'majority' assumes that its culture is the 'natural' culture of the whole society, its language dominates the private as well as the public sphere.

This privileged position of a group generally stems from access to the state apparatus. Race then becomes a political category fixing a well-defined distinction between groups. The power of the state manifests itself in different ways that vary from what can be called 'racial definition', to the managing of opportunities for employment, housing and schooling. The state assumes a major role in alleviating or exacerbating racial disadvantage by the policies which it adopts. Today, legislation affecting migrant workers from Eastern Europe and Africa into Western Europe is one of the major problems faced by the European Union. It puts into question moral and economic principles.

The 'majority' has the power to decide upon the status of minority groups' members. The 'majority' regards as natural its capacity to determine the minority's status and perceives its power as grounded in its unquestionable superiority. Patronage and condescension are likely to emerge in a context in which those considered inferior play an active part in the established economic structure of production. A cheap, unproblematic labour force willing to perform any type of job and passively accepting submission is easier to tolerate.

In time of crisis minorities receive harsher treatment. They are blamed for the misfortunes affecting the whole society. They are considered guilty because of their 'inefficiency', 'laziness', 'lack of culture', 'propensity to crime', 'arrogance' or 'economic success'. Any excuse seems appropriate to emphasize the 'difference' and negatively charge it. Racism gains recruits in hard times when the pre-eminent status of a group is under threat. But an unstable economy is not the only feature which may favour racism. There exist ideological factors capable of awakening alarm among the 'dominant'. The expansion of democratic and egalitarian discourses challenges the indisputability of racism. Globalization breaks the isolation of cultures and peoples. Discrimination cannot be tacit any more. The images of, and news about, what a democratic society should look like and the diffusion of ideas about human rights question the existence of forms of power grounded on racist exploitation.

Racism and gender

Different articulations of racism correspond to social class and gender categories. This assertion aims to clarify two aspects commonly neglected when discussing racism: the existence of intra-class and intra-race divisions, and the different position of women in virtue of their class, culture and ethnicity. Marxist feminism has recognized that as a social relation gender is constructed partly through class and economic relations and that at the empirical level the experience of subordination and oppression varies in form within different class and economic contexts. However, as Anthias and Yuval-Davis argue, 'most of this work has not been able to integrate into its analysis differentiation structured either by racism or by ethnicity.'[9] In fact, Black feminism regards Western feminism as racist because it 'fails to take as central the anti-racist struggle, which ought to be within the parameters of a social movement concerned with the ways women have been oppressed'.[10]

Gender and race are both underpinned by a supposedly 'natural' relation which assigns different qualities and needs to individuals and 'justifies' inequalities. Class, gender and race reflect power structures within a given society and play a crucial role in the constitution of individual identity.

The idea of race has changed substantially under the influence of the New Right. Prejudice is given new arguments. New racism exploits the 'naturalness' of race divisions by arguing that 'it is natural for people of one kind to group together and natural for them to be wary of, or even antagonistic towards, outsiders'.[11] Gordon and Klug deny that this entails a belief in the innate superiority of one group above others. Human nature, in their view, binds similar people together for innate reasons, and groups that are 'different' are rejected as part of a natural instinct to protect one's own.[12]

Racism and nationalism

Racism is a doctrine of denial of political, civic and social rights. It means hatred of the different. Racism and nationalism offer radically different messages. Racism emerged as a doctrine of exclusion to legitimize domination of phenotypically diverse groups, and it has proved crucial in the creation and reproduction of class-structures grounded on the subordination of those defined as inferior by nature. Racism does not cut across national boundaries, it determines the relation between groups that live together in a compartmentalized society.

Racists want to dominate the territory they occupy, which can be either the result of a relatively recent conquest or the land they have occupied from immemorial times. In the former case they ignore the autochthonous peoples' right to continue living and working freely in the land of their ancestors. In the latter, which is usually the case in non-colonial territories, they aim to stop the contamination of a land and people presented as superior. Nationalism wants to regenerate the nation, make its culture flourish and its people feel engaged in a common project that transcends their own life-spans. Nationalism is about building, dreaming and working for a better future for the new generations. Racism does not attempt to construct anything.

Nationalism and racism exhibit fundamental oppositions, but it is obvious that certain formulations of nationalism have been in the past and still are associated with racism. The so-called dark side of nationalism comes into the light when those struggling to promote and develop their nation decide to do so without respecting the right to exist and evolve of other nations, in particular their neighbours. The great weakness of nationalism stems precisely from its being a word used in the description of such different attitudes and aims. This type of nationalism possesses a particular way of seeing the basic relation between 'us' and 'them' and uses it in the construction of national identity. The 'other' is not someone who makes us aware of our own particularities, someone we can learn from, respect, live with and take as a point of reference in the construction of our own identity. This nationalism sees in the 'other' a potential or factual enemy, but above all someone inferior. This is the case when racism is incorporated into a nationalist discourse. Nazism defended the creation of a 'greater' Germany. The extermination of those portrayed as the cause of German problems was justified by citing their racial inferiority. The other's existence was perceived as posing a threat to Aryan excellence. Contamination had to be avoided at any price. Less extreme cases are racist behaviour against North African temporary labourers in Spain and France, and against Eastern European and Turkish migrants in contemporary Germany.

In post-colonial states, racism is a residue from a past in which European superiority was officially recognized (by Europeans, of course). Racism accompanied a certain type of nationalism inspired by the idea of empire beyond the frontiers of the metropolis. In former colonies racists show some sort of nostalgia for a golden past in which their pre-eminence remained unchallenged, for a time in which they could even feel morally satisfied by bringing civilization to 'barbarian' peoples. Colonizers thought indigenous peoples should be grateful to them since, in a way, to be exploited was a privilege; it meant being in touch with an evidently 'superior' culture. Racists, in these areas, seek to sustain a class-structure they benefit from. They employ a nationalist discourse in an attempt to legitimize their claims and are usually confronted by emerging vernacular nationalisms.

Fascism

A certain brand of nationalism is at the core of the fascist discourse. This section provides a definition of fascism that will serve as a vantage point for the study of its psychological bases and its link with certain aspects of nationalism. The text refers to the fascist regimes of the 1922–45 period, but wants to stress the actuality of fascist ideas, which are still very much alive in neo-Nazi and neo-Fascist groups today.

Linz defines fascism as an anti-movement. In his view, anti-liberalism, anti-parliamentarism, anti-semitism (except in Italy), anti-communism, partial anti-capitalism and anti-bourgeoisism, anti-clericalism or at least non-clericalism define fascism.[13] All these anti-positions, combined with exacerbating nationalist sentiments, lead in many cases to pan-nationalist ideas which in the past posed a challenge to the existing states and account for much of the aggressive expansionist foreign policy of some fascist regimes.[14]

The cult of the elite, of youth, of maleness, of force and violence, the revolt against the nationalism of the Enlightenment and the advocacy of political authoritarianism are the elements that complete the portrait of fascism. In Sternhell's view, every one of these elements was already in existence in August 1914 and had a history going back to the 1880s.[15]

Fascism's essence, Dandeker argues, 'is the attempt to abolish political disputes; it is the (unsuccessful) final solution of the problems of politics.'[16] According to Eley, fascism involved a qualitative departure from existing conservative practice, replacing traditional notions of hierarchy with corporatist notions of social organization combined with fresh ideas of a centrally directed authoritarian state, and a new kind of regulated, multi-class, integrated national-economic structure.[17] But, above all, fascism stood for an ideal of national concentration in which allegiance to the nation liquidated all forms of sectional identification. The Italian Gorgolini wrote in 1921: 'Fascism is the religion of the fatherland.'[18]

The EEC's Committee of Inquiry into the Rise of Fascism and Racism in Europe defined fascism as 'a nationalistic attitude essentially hostile to the principles of democracy, to the rule of law and to the fundamental rights and freedoms, as well as the irrational exaltation of a particular community, in relation to which people outside it are systematically excluded'.[19]

In the 1920s fascism revealed itself as a utopian revolutionary movement attempting to overthrow the existing order. However, when successful, it proceeded to assume a reactionary and oppressive character. The economic crisis and the discontent caused by the conditions of the Treaty of Versailles after the First World War, favoured the spread of the new ideology in Germany and Italy. Fascism provided many millions of people with a more meaningful involvement than representative parliamentary government. Ex-servicemen played a key role in the maturing of fascism. As depositaries of the national heritage and guardians of the nation's greatness, they considered themselves the bearers of a special mission. Their aim was to regenerate the country, to refashion the world in their own heroic image. In Mosse's words: 'the crucial role which the war experience played in National Socialism is well enough known. The war was a "lovely dream" and a "miracle of achievement", as one Nazi children's book put it. Any death in war was a hero's death and thus the true fulfilment of life.'[20]

The regeneration of the nation is one of the major objectives of any nationalist movement. In the case of fascism, belonging to the same nation is the quality that unites all citizens. The construction of the community stands above other sources of identity, such as class. The regeneration of the national community is a simple and successful message that usually implies the ethnic or cultural superiority of the reborn nation over certain peoples and cultures judged inferior. This was the case in Nazi Germany and still is within the now emerging neo-fascist groups in Europe. 'Fascists', Griffin argues, 'typically imagine themselves in the front line of an historical and cultural battle to turn back the tide of mediocrity and loss of vitality and so reinstate the exceptional, the outstanding, the heroic as the driving force of history'.[21] Fascism crops up as an outlet for idealism and self-sacrifice. Its undemocratic character expresses itself in the influence exerted on its ideology by elitist theories of society such as those of Pareto, Sorel, Mosca or Nieztsche. Fascism is an attitude towards life that involves all aspects of the individual.

Fascism offers an alternative modernism. A number of fascist movements romanticized pre-industrial social structures, and rejected urban, industrial, commercial values and lifestyles. As Linz notes, in their rejection of cosmopolitanism, commercialism and consumerism, and their appeal for a return to nature, they coincided with the peasant-ist ideologists, certain brands of populism and powerful intellectual currents that at the turn of the century were particularly articulate in Germany.[22] However, fascism did not seek to destroy the process of industrialization, on the contrary, it deliberately furthered it in order to increase the country's might and prosperity. The commitment to military preparedness, the concern for planning for collective purposes pushed fascists towards a policy of industrialization. The Futurists, and Mussolini with them, were fascinated by technology. The key question concerning the modernism of fascist ideology derives from its treatment of industrialization as a technological advance. Fascism subordinated industrialism to an anti-industrial ideology and denied it the possibility of leading to a new perception of the world. Con-temporary nationalism shows a similar ambivalence when dealing with the signs of modernity. The regeneration or rebirth of the nation usually means looking back to the pristine and golden past. However, nation-alism needs to face the future and prepare the nation to compete and escape backwardness. This process involves the reappropriation of technology and industry, and the reinterpretation of tradition.

Fascism and race

Diverse forms of racism pervade fascist ideology. They emanate from the fascist attempt to generate a sense of uniqueness, a self-centred community that rejects cosmopolitanism and ethnic difference. Scholars of fascism differ in the role attributed to the racist component in the German and Italian regimes. O'Sullivan mentions three basic differences between Hitler's and Mussolini's movements that can be summarized as follows:

1 Whereas Nazism rested on the doctrine of race, Italian ideolo-gists always stressed the non-biological, voluntarist basis of their movement.
2 Divergence of tone. Although the Italian Fascist movement prided itself on the brutality of the squads, the policies of the regime were mild by comparison with those associated with Nazism.
3 Different degree of success in penetrating the national life of the two countries.

Hitler and Mussolini put forward opposing conceptions of race and its relation with politics. Thus while Hitler wrote: 'The State is only the vessel and the race is what it contains. The vessel can have meaning . . . only if it preserves and safeguards the contents. Otherwise it is worthless . . . from this it follows that it is not the task of the state to create human capabilities, but only to assure free scope for the capabilities that already exist.'[23] Mussolini identified the nation and the state. In his view the nation represented the material and spiritual interests of a specific historical community. The state was its juridical incarnation.[24] In fascist thought the state, as the ultimate depositary of force, was charged with sustaining the norms governing individual and collective behaviour. For fascism, the state made community life possible and was infinitely superior to both the individuals and organizations of which the national community was composed. Gregor concludes that fascism 'identified society with the nation, the nation with the state, and economic activity with political activity'.[25] O'Sullivan emphasizes that although frequent references to race may indeed be found in Italian nationalist literature both before and after the advent of fascism, the word was largely a rhetorical one without any of the biological connotations which were vital to it in Nazi usage. Mussolini was able to use religion as a source of unity. The Lateran Pact (1929) implied the Papacy's support for the Fascist movement.[26]

Mosse supports the idea that emphasis upon race conferred on Nazism a dimension lacking in Italian Fascism. In his view, 'Nazism and anti-semitism were not a necessary component of fascism and certainly not of those parts of the movement that looked for their model to Italy, where, until 1938, racism did not exist'.[27] Gentile, one of the ideologists of fascism, rejected biological determinism. The publication of *The Manifesto of Fascist Racism* in 1938 responded to Mussolini's introduction of Nazi-style racism into fascism, as an accompaniment to his regime's increasing diplomatic and military alliance with Nazi Germany.

Many of the distinctive features of National Socialism mostly derived from the cultural heritage of Germany and Austria, which in the nineteenth century cultivated some of the elements described by the term *völkisch* which, in turn, facilitated the presence of racism within the Nazi movement. The strong nationalist component of fascism gave special emphasis to national culture and history. In the case of Germany this favoured the introduction of biological difference as a way to classify people. In spite of this, fascists saw Nazism as a kindred movement even when distrusting German power. Linz argues that 'conflicts between fascist powers, different emphases in their ideology and policies are not an argument against the use of a broader category of fascism.'[28] Karl Bracher and Renzo de Felice also maintain that it is possible to establish some common features conforming to a minimum fascism. Sternhell stands in opposition to this assertion. According to him, Nazism cannot be treated as a mere variant of fascism: its emphasis on biological determinism rules out all efforts to deal with it as such. Sternhell argues that anti-semitism was used by National Socialism as the perfect tool for the integration of the proletariat within the national community and had the advantage of rallying the petty bourgeoisie in danger of proletarization.[29] Corradini established a distinction between 'proletarian' and 'bourgeois' nations, and declared that nationalism desired to be for the whole nation what socialism had been for the proletariat.[30] The description of Italy as a 'proletarian' nation exploited by more advantaged nations provided fascists with an effective argument in order to mobilize Italians, who, as Gregor argues, 'could give themselves over to the defence of the fatherland ... to their collective, mutual advantage and in pursuit of justice'.[31]

Fascism and ritual

Nazism considered the state as the emanation of the *Volk* and sought the preservation and enhancement of the Aryan race. Mussolini saw the state as the creator of the nation, the Italian Fascist discourse aimed at the construction of a new man, a man of the future: 'the Homo fascistus'.

Fascism implied a new style in politics. One of the most prominent and distinctive features of fascism was the use of symbols, ceremonies and rituals. A world of sacred objects was created and their worship efficiently organized. The leader (*Führer, duce, caudillo*), the party and the *Volk* (interpreted variously as the people, the nation, or the race) were at the centre of the new cult. The initial style of fascist movements, many of their symbols, parades, banners and even programmatic positions were invented by d'Annunzio in the struggle for Fiume.[32]

The emerging secular religion of fascism appealed to the sentiments of the people who by uttering the same cry and marching along singing the same anthems felt their identity merge into that of the group. Belonging to the same nation erased all other sources of identification. Emotional participation in the mythically constructed nation was above everything else and had the power to demand the supreme sacrifice:

the willingness to give up one's life for the common ideals signalled by the leader who embodied not only the party, but the whole nation.

Mussolini knew the work of Pareto and Le Bon's *Psychology of Crowds*. Both of these thinkers criticized the Marxist neglect of 'paralogical' or 'sentimental' motives affecting collective behaviour. In 1903 Mussolini stressed that 'sentiments are the dynamic motives of human actions', pointing to the 'sentiment of solidarity' as crucial in moving men into war.[33] The Nazis in their attempt to propagate and strengthen their doctrine among the *Volk* created some Nazi ceremonies to rival the Christian Churches' Sunday services and their christening, marriage and funeral rites. Alfred Rosenberg, appointed by Hitler as plenipotentiary for the spiritual and ideological education of the Party wrote in 1934: 'a *Weltanschauung* could not be expressed properly in only principles or needs and had to "take on the form of a cult".'[34]

Fascism and gender

The role conferred on women within fascist society was restricted to the production and rearing of children. Women were mothers and wives who had to look after the purity of the race. Fascism encouraged high birth rates to increase the power of the nation. The camaraderie and qualities of life in wartime were reproduced in the squads and groups organized by the fascist parties. Male strength and beauty, youth[35] and a new emphasis upon fitness together with an aggressive virility and an *élan vital* stood as crucial elements in the configuration of the masculine prototype. The cult of physical strength, life, health and blood was combined with a contempt for intellectuals. The notion that feelings can be shared was implicit in the prominent role conferred upon public gatherings addressed to wide audiences inflamed by the charisma of the leader. The discussion of arguments could only appeal to an insignificant number of people. The strategy of convincing and moving the masses stemmed from the power of a discourse touching upon their inner feelings and sentiments.

The fascist new world was to be built by an elite rejecting a boring and easy life and ready to engage in a lively and dangerous experience. Masculinity was equated with strength, sexuality, violence and brutality.[36] Femininity meant a passive surrender to the force of men and the acceptance of a key role as caretakers of children, the elderly, ex-servicemen, and men in general, although the task of women was substantially altered during the Second World War, when they played a vital part in maintaining industrial production. But fascism constructed a new appealing model of masculinity that excluded women; no woman could be found among key party figures. The fascist leader could only be thought of as a man.

Fascism and nationalism

Both contemporary nationalism and fascism have a tendency to evolve into mass movements. The existence of a devoted elite is fundamental to nationalism. The presence of a charismatic leader is crucial to the success of the movement in arousing the masses. The cult of the leader lies at the centre of fascist ideology and brought an entirely new structure of organization for the political movements of this century. The first and most important of the leader's tasks is to serve as a symbolic embodiment of the myth which shapes the historical destiny of his people. The leader is always a **man** devoted to arousing emotions and encouraging his listeners to 'live out' the fascist myth rather than to examine it critically. The fascist leader, as O'Sullivan argues, 'must ensure his movement is free from the disputes over the relationship between theory and practice which bedevil other ideologies. To achieve this internal harmony he must claim to be infallible in all matters of fascist faith, morality and politics.'[37] He distinguishes three major functions of the leader principle (*Führerprinzip*):

1 To give embodiment to the fascist myth.
2 To provide the organizational basis of the movement/regime with which fascism seeks to replace the state order.
3 To create a new theory of legitimacy.

The leader principle proved effective in the inception of emotional solidarity and the maintenance of a fanatical spirit of loyalty and self-sacrifice amongst the Nazi elite. But as a general principle of social organization, it turned out to be both administratively inefficient and ideologically counterproductive.[38]

Carl Schmitt supplies the most sophisticated theory of Nazism. He detaches himself from *völkisch* rhetoric and legitimizes the infallibility of the leader. In his view the leader embodies the people who possess no independent existence (and hence no will) apart from him. The leader's claim to power is based on the belief that he intuitively understands and articulates the real will of the people. The leader keeps a direct and quasi-religious relationship with his movement in order to externalize the will of the people rejecting, at least in principle, institutional forms of any kind. 'Schmitt's analysis implies', as O'Sullivan argues, that 'the fascist leader cannot be regarded as a dictator, in the traditional sense of that term.'[39]

Nationalism contributed to liberation and emancipation movements in the nineteenth century. At that time nationalism was basically a progressive doctrine inseparably connected with democratic and universalist values inherited from the French Revolution. The fascist appropriation of nationalism revealed the 'dark side' of a movement which never recovered from the impact of fascist ideas. Nationalism responded to the urgent desire to transcend anxieties and escape confusion of a population who had just suffered a war and were living through the effects of an economic crisis. The dream of re-creating a sense of community among the members of the nation and the infusion of a neo-idealism centred in a new ideology capable of absorbing all aspects of life stood as a seductive option. Fascism, above all a nationalist movement, provided many millions of people with a meaningful involvement. It used the national community as a 'natural', 'genuine' entity with its own organic strength and life, analogous to nature.

Fascism as nationalism pursued the linkage of past and present, offering individuals the opportunity to engage in a common project for the future of their nation, an entity to which they belonged and which transcended them. By integrating the proletariat into the national community, fascism managed to wipe out the identification effected by democracy of the nation with its bourgeoisie. As Sternhell points out, this implied the restoration of the authenticity, integrity and wholeness of the national community. At the same time, socialism was transcended in National Socialism.[40] For, as he writes, 'from now onwards the future would be shaped by struggle not between the proletarian and capitalist classes, but between the proletarian and plutocratic nations. Instead of a class, it was the nation now that was going to set the course of history, as the agent of progress and civilisation.'[41] The nation as a complex entity based upon attachment to a concrete territory, common historical past, values and culture, showed once more the force of its inhabitants' common consciousness and their will to decide upon their political destiny. The nation revealed itself as the primary focus of loyalty.

For fascists, the nation is natural and stands above class. However, this assertion also contains the idea of the individual as a function of group life. Individuals are considered social animals. For Gentile 'man has existence only insofar as he is sustained and determined by the community.'[42] In Mussolini's words, 'man is only man by virtue of the spiritual process to which he contributes as a member of the family, the social group, the nation, and in function of history to which all nations bring their contributions.'[43]

Fascism as well as nationalism is based upon the drawing of boundaries between insiders and outsiders. Carl Schmitt's theory describing the political relationship between friend and foe takes to unthinkable lengths the opposition between 'us' and 'them'. In his view, even the existence of the other is perceived as an ontological or existential threat to own's life. The foe must therefore be destroyed in order to protect one's own distinct existence. Friend and foe refer, in their political sense, not to individuals but to collectivities. The conflict between them must itself inevitably be a total one which only ends when the foe is annihilated. In Schmitt's theory the other is an enemy that can only be reduced if eliminated. It is not a matter of fixing boundaries but rather an attempt to eradicate all those that are different, whatever their attitudes or ideas.[44]

The search for community is a recurrent feature of modern societies. In time of crisis, the new brotherhood of blood put forward by fascism proved successful in trying to mitigate the isolation of modern individuals. Fascism allowed people to be close to each other and cut across status and class barriers. Fascism in its actions, as Linz stresses, 'satisfied both the desire for the heroic deed of romantic individualism and the desire to submerge in a collective enterprise'.[45]

5
Nations without a State

In chapter two I referred to a nation as a 'human group conscious of forming a community, sharing a common culture, attached to a clearly demarcated territory, having a common past and a common project for the future and claiming the right to rule itself'. A nation should be distinguished from an ethnic group whose members, in spite of sharing in some unspecified way a common origin and manifold cultural, historical and territorial ties, do not put forward specific political demands.

One of the elements currently conjoining to change the shape of the world is the unexpected impetus gained by the appeal to ethnic ties among the members of certain communities lacking their own political institutions. We are witnessing a process by means of which collective cultural units with variable degrees of cohesion are intensifying their awareness of forming a group.

This chapter explores the ways in which a nationalist discourse is articulated in nations without a state. It first studies the processes leading to 'national awareness' and the shift from cultural to political demands, offering a systematic analysis of the strategies employed by national minorities in resisting the homogenizing policies of the states containing them.

As a preliminary to any attempt to indicate which are the common features of nationalism in nations lacking a state of their own, it is necessary to emphasize that substantially different political scenarios emerge from the specific character of the nation-states within which such nations are included. At least four different situations may be distinguished:

1 A nation-state may acknowledge the 'cultural differences' of its minority or minorities, without allowing more than the cultivation and promotion of their own culture and the maintenance of some deep-rooted elements of the socio-cultural tradition. Britain's attitude towards Scotland and Wales could be posed as an example. The predominance of the Presbyterian Church and a separate educational system in Scotland, and the recent concern about increasing the presence of the Welsh language and culture in day-to-day activities are not accompanied so far by any political measures leading to devolution. Thus, Scotland and Wales, although being equal partners with England within Britain, are forced to go down to London to solve most of their domestic problems.

2 A certain degree of autonomy within the state is the option faced by nations such as Catalonia and the Basque Country within the Autonomous Communities System created in Spain after Franco's dictatorship. Both minorities have their own Statute of Autonomy regulating their status within the framework of the 1978 Constitution; they possess their own parliament, government and president elected in the regional election, and enjoy the right to decide on a fair number of issues whose competency has been transferred to them from the Spanish central government in Madrid.

3 The situation of Quebec and Flanders as nations integrated within a federation permits the highest degree of self-determination for nations without a state. They have benefited from wide political powers to decide about their social, economic and political life without actually becoming independent. In both cases, however, a federal structure does not seem to satisfy completely the aspirations of significant sectors of the population, including nationalist parties which advocate separation and the constitution of sovereign states.

4 A further category covers nations completely lacking recognition from the state which contains them. In these cases, the state actively employs itself in formulating policies aiming at the elimination of difference within its territory. Violence in the form of military control is sometimes used against national minorities resisting the state. Palestinians living in Israel were a clear example of this situation up to the recent agreement to confer a certain amount of autonomy on Palestine, while the Tibetan and Kurdish peoples are currently struggling to obtain recognition from the Chinese government, and from the different states amongst which the Kurdish land is partitioned.

Processes of 'national awareness'

The common feature lying behind any minority's nationalist movement calling for greater autonomy or independence is dissatisfaction
with its current situation. The feeling that they could benefit from
distancing themselves from the state that includes them is commonly
based upon discontent about security, economic prosperity or political
participation.

Radical changes altering the traditional shape of the nation-state are
contributing to the configuration of a new scenario within which new
states are emerging. The traditional definition of the state as the institution which controls the means of violence within a clearly demarcated territory is no longer accurate. There are international and
supranational organizations which possess high-technology weapons
capable not only of threatening the nation-state's power but also of
paralysing it. In addition, the economic prosperity of the nation-state
no longer solely relies on the ability of its rulers. International forces
are involved, and some minorities get the feeling that they could do
better on their own. Small units can be functional in the current world.
Relatively small size and population do not seem to be an obstacle to
the constitution of a new independent nation-state. The recent independence achieved by the Baltic Republics can be taken as an example.

A further element contributing to the spread of nationalism among
minorities is the collapse of the state's institutions. The failure to fulfil
people's basic needs, and the non-existence of satisfactory alternative
structures, are key factors to an understanding of the unexpected proliferation of nationalist movements in the former Soviet Union, where
new state structures are in the process of being established, but are not
yet able to provide for the security and well-being of their constituents.

The claim that the state is an 'independent authority' or a 'cir-
cumscribed impartial power' accountable to its citizens, a notion that,
as Held argues, lies at the centre of the self-image or ideology of
the modern state, is today fundamentally flawed.[1] The nation-state
is caught up in profound processes of transformation prompted by
alterations in the conditions of its existence *vis-à-vis* a changing world
economy and international order. Nation-states have lost aspects of
their sovereignty and are forced to face patterns of increasing global
interconnections. The nationalism of minorities and the proliferation
of supranational organizations such as the EU are also contributing to
the transformation of the nature of the nation-state.

However, the age of the nation-state is by no means exhausted.

States will continue to be prime political actors, and their strength and resilience will not be undermined in the foreseeable future. States are reluctant to submit their disputes with other states to arbitration by a 'superior authority', be it the United Nations, an international court or any other international body. They do not renounce their intra-state monopolies of violence and whenever necessary fuel nationalism as a means to sustain their legitimacy. The aim of most nationalist movements in nations without a state consists in creating their own state and entering the international nation-state system. This must be understood as a sign of the nation-state's resilience and protagonism.

National awareness usually begins with the activities of small groups of intellectuals struggling to maintain and recover the minority's culture and, when it exists, language. In these early stages, the gap between an 'enlightened' minority and the masses is extremely wide, and the chances for the minority's cultural expansion are slim. The actions of these elites lie at the edge of legality, and are sometimes completely clandestine in states that do not tolerate diversity within them.

The expansion of ideas about the culture, history and, in many cases, political independence enjoyed by a minority attached to a concrete territory, when linked to dissatisfaction about its current situation, may lead to a shift from simply cultural to political aspirations. The will to intervene in decision-making processes and the right to have access to sufficient resources to improve the life of the minority and promote its culture occupy the centre of the demands for autonomy.

The nationalist demands of minorities are likely to be perceived as a threat to the state's integrity. In some cases the state yields to pressure and transforms its nature in such a way that the minority is satisfied with democratic reforms aimed at the implementation of democracy, obtains more political, economic, cultural or administrative autonomy within existing institutional arrangements, or achieves the status of an independent political entity within a new federal structure.

However, there are cases in which the state's active engagement in the annihilation of the specific identity of a national minority produces a radically different situation. A progressive estrangement from the state pervades the minority except for those members, usually belonging to the high bourgeoisie, who renounce their national identity in order to protect their status by defending their class interests. The homogenizing policy imposed by the state encounters diverse types of reactions leading to the preservation of the minority's distinctiveness. A national minority under threat develops various sorts of counter-strategies to reject the forced uniformity dictated by the state. Such counter-strategies are the result of, and have the capacity to increase, the national awareness of a given group. Earlier on I distinguished between armed struggle and cultural resistance as major counter-strategies against enforced homogeneity. I shall now expand on these particular points.

Cultural resistance

Cultural resistance is the use of all sorts of symbols of the national minority's identity in the public as well as in the private sphere, ranging from isolated and risky actions to activities enlisting massive support. Such actions symbolically break the state's control and make it clear that there exists some form of discontent among the population. In the private domain, resistance is primarily carried out by the family. The minority's language and culture are learned at home and in many cases they can only be put into practice within restricted groups determined by family or friendship ties.

I distinguish four major forms of opposition within the public domain: 'symbolic actions', 'interference actions', 'elite actions' and 'solidarity actions'. By 'symbolic action', I mean a single and usually isolated action carried out by a small group or even a single individual whose main objective is to break the control of the public space in the hands of the oppressive regime. Graffiti and flag displaying should be included in this category. Symbolic actions are usually performed in the street and addressed to all witnesses who are present at the time.

By 'interference actions' I refer to single actions executed by small groups during the course of public events. The task of such actions is to challenge the regime at its core and disrupt rituals and ceremonies whose aim is precisely to prove that homogeneity and control have been achieved. 'Interference actions' imply a high degree of risk, since security measures designed to prevent any sort of disturbance are strongly implemented on such occasions. 'Interference actions' envisage a double reception: on the one hand, they are addressed to those attending the public event, but on the other, they seek the attention of 'alien' observers such as the international press or foreign representatives, partially or completely unaware of the minority's situation.

'Elite actions' are carried out by a small but devoted intelligentsia. Their objective is the maintenance and, if at all possible, the development of the minority's high culture. Opposition movements take advantage of all possible breaches to advance their resistance actively. When the process of national awareness has reached the masses there is an increase in the number of 'solidarity actions'. By 'solidarity action', I mean an action that is usually prepared or instigated by a small elite but whose aim is to mobilize a larger number of people, to achieve mass participation. The objective of a 'solidarity action' is to show the strength of the national minority by focusing upon a particular demand and presenting it as something that cannot be denied due to the massive support it receives. A fundamental change concerning the context in which actions are performed distinguishes 'solidarity actions' from both 'symbolic' and 'interference actions'. The latter attempt to break the control of the public sphere in the context of a highly repressive discipline surrounding all public activities. The former can only take place when a relative attenuation of the oppressive nature of the regime allows some breaches to be made and the population then dares to gather together challenging the power of the state. The two million people forming a human chain stretching from Estonia to Lithuania in August 1989 to show their condemnation of the Molotov–Ribbentrop Pact which assigned the Baltic states to the Soviet Union, or the one-million-strong mass demonstration in Barcelona on 11 September 1977 in an attempt to vindicate a Statute of Autonomy for Catalonia, are cases in point.

Armed struggle

The right to self-determination and eventual independence of a nation without a state is usually seen as somewhat problematic. In many cases antagonistic national groups are not able to agree on new constitutional arrangements or a peaceful separation. They reject assimilation, and are not satisfied with cultural resistance. Armed struggle is then regarded as the only alternative in order to gain political autonomy. Violence adopts many forms when related to the conflict caused by the nationalist demands of the different nations or parts of nations integrated within a single state. The terminology used to describe it varies depending on the speaker's standpoint.

Armed struggle emerges as a reaction to the state's repression. This can be social, economic, political, and in extreme circumstances have a military character. The strength and means of the minority will determine the intensity of its response. 'Total war' and 'target attacks' are the two options available to the national minority that has decided to employ force as a means to change its status. 'Target attacks' refer to attacks against soft, high-value targets belonging to or representing the state's institutions, property or territory. 'Target attacks' seek the attention of the international and national media and aim to show the vulnerability of the state, its incapacity to predict and control the use of violence by agents other than its own. The activities of the IRA, ETA or *Sendero Luminoso* could be mentioned as examples. A new strategy used by some groups in 'target attacks' consists of targeting a public place regardless of the allegiance and characteristics of possible victims. The effectiveness of this type of attack lies in the amount of media coverage it can obtain.

'Total war' is a civil war between members of the same state belonging to antagonistic national communities. 'Total war' is usually fought by recently formed or recently augmented militias composed of ordinary citizens. When total war involves the nation dominating the state and a national minority trying to break away from it, the militia of the minority is confronted by the military forces representing the state. With no foreign intervention it is unlikely that the minority will take over and win the confrontation unless it faces an extremely weak state. Intra-state wars do not tend to use high-technology weapons and almost always involve deliberate, systematic attacks on civilians to weaken the military resources on which adversaries can draw. A significant feature of 'total war' is that civilian populations of warring groups are often intermingled. When battle lines exist, they often cut through cities, towns, even neighbourhoods. Control over particular pieces of territory is of major importance in a 'total war'. To secure complete territorial control, militias seek to drive out civilians from other groups and force them to leave their homes and property. The war in the former Yugoslavia exemplifies the horrific practices of ethnic cleansing involving forced expulsions and the systematic slaughter of civilians.

'Total wars' often generate staggering numbers of refugees precisely because they are based upon systematic attacks on civilian populations. Brown discerns six possible problems posed by increasing numbers of refugees seeking asylum in neighbouring countries.

1 Offering sanctuary to refugees can invite reprisals thereby drawing the host country into the conflict.
2 If refugees flee to neighbouring countries where large numbers of their compatriots live, the latter can also become involved in the conflict, thereby widening the war.
3 Refugees impose tremendous economic costs on host states.
4 Refugees can be seen as potential threats to the cultural identity of host states, especially when they form large communities.

5   Refugees can become political forces in host countries, particularly regarding foreign policy issues relating to their homeland.
6   Finally, when refugee problems pose threats to 'international peace and security', as they often do, the United Nations has a right, if not an obligation, to consider intervening in the crisis.[2]

One of the major changes affecting national minorities engaging in total war or target attacks in this age of globalization is the immediate transmission of the images and ideas underlying their struggle to most of the world's population. Thus the success of a national minority in attaining recognition, autonomy or independence and the non-violent response of a state to its minorities' claims in one part of the world might encourage nationalist movements in other areas to put forward similar demands.

Political solutions to the nationalism of minorities

National minorities exhibit changing degrees of self-consciousness that impact upon the character and intensity of their demands. Political autonomy and independence are the two major objectives sought by nations included within an alien state's territory.

Once again it is crucial to stress that a nation without a state can achieve substantially different levels of political autonomy. Note that the word 'autonomy' itself is subjected to differing interpretations according to the ideology and political context within which it is employed. For instance, the right to autonomy of the nationalities and regions forming Spain materialized into what is called the Autonomous Communities System (*el Sistema Autonómico*). Yet, while Catalonia, the Basque Country and Galicia, which had ratified statutes of autonomy during the Second Republic, could immediately initiate the process towards full autonomy (*régimen autonómico pleno*), other regions had to fulfil a five-year 'restricted autonomy' period (*régimen autonómico restringido o mínimo*) before initiating it. Once full autonomy is achieved, however, the Constitution makes no distinction between the 'communities'. Instead, it equalizes nationalities with a strong sense of identity based upon common culture, language and past, with newly and sometimes artificially created 'communities'. The Autonomous System responded to pressure exerted primarily by the Basque Country and Catalonia. Both minorities felt that they had not only the right but also the power to press for a political solution to their claims for self-determination.

Once the new model of the Spanish state was established by the

Constitution, the implementation of the Autonomous Communities System became a pressing matter. The question arose of whether it would turn into a simple administrative decentralization device or symbolize the recognition of the particular cultural and political aspirations of national minorities.

The 1978 Spanish Constitution set down the basis for a new agenda which established how national minorities should be treated. Since 1978, however, conflict between the communities and the central government has been raging to the point where it seems to be a necessary forerunner of negotiations and agreements between both political institutions.

A constitution that strives to reconcile unity within the state's territory with a fair amount of political autonomy to the nations it contains, faces tension and conflict. This is so because the clash between two entities which seek the same objective, that is, the creation and enhancement of the nation, is inevitable unless one of the following options is adopted. The first requires the transformation of the state into a purely administrative device which co-ordinates the policies of its different nations and parts of nations. The second assumes that the minority decides not to fuel a nationalism that could eventually lead to independence, and to function as part of the state. This involves the cultivation of difference within certain limits and assumes a careful calculation not to break the equilibrium between a strong sense of identity and the acceptance of the state's structure.

Federalism presents itself as a system that offers a considerable amount of political, cultural and economic freedom to the areas adopting it. Federalism, as Gagnon argues, indicates a commitment to a contractual arrangement between political units that decide to create a new political space.[3] The appeal to form a federation to respond to the nationalist claims of a nation without a state implies the state's decision to recast its structure and consider the nation in question as sovereign or quasi-sovereign since federalism exists only if, as King stresses, formed by equal partners as free to withdraw from, as to enter into, such an association.[4]

There are cases in which the state yields to the enormous pressure exerted by a national minority and puts forward a federalist structure in an attempt to satisfy the minority's claim for further autonomy and avoid secession. This is the case in Belgium which was set up as a unitary state formed by a southern French-speaking part (Wallonia) and a northern Dutch-speaking area (Flanders) in 1831. Belgium was first officially referred to as a federal state in 1988, after a process of constitutional reform initiated by the Flemish Catholic premier Gaston

Eyskens. The constitutional reform provided for limited cultural autonomy along language lines, while excluding education and finance.
In 1988 the constitutional reformers worked out a strikingly original
concept, since 'not only do the constituent parts differ thoroughly at
the economic, social, ideological and linguistic-cultural levels, but there
is also an incredible degree of complexity and asymmetry among the
newly created institutions themselves, as witness the extreme case
of the political structures in the Brussels region.'[5] However, federal
decentralization does not seem to satisfy the nationalist demands of
the Flemish fully.

In a similar way, the Canadian federation has not managed to halt
the pro-independence movement in Quebec. In the 1960s people in
Quebec began to complain about the limitations imposed upon the
province by the federal system. Notwithstanding significant constitutional changes and the explicit recognition of Canada as a bilingual
and bicultural society following Prime Minister Pierre Trudeau's lead,
the Quebec provincial government refused to ratify the Constitution
Act of 1982. The Quebecois demanded the right to be recognized as a
'distinct society' within Canada's federal system. The 1987 Meech Lake
Accord which met the Quebecois demand failed after going through
a long process. A second proposal, that was not only to acknowledge
Quebec as a distinct society but also to contemplate aboriginal rights,
was put forward in 1992. The Charlottetown Agreement, despite
emerging as the outcome of a mutual understanding between the
federal Prime Minister, the ten provincial premiers and the leaders
of various indigenous groups, was rejected in a referendum held in
October 1992.[6] Belgium's and Canada's futures remain unclear. In
both cases compelling nationalist movements are challenging the
unity of the state and might end up prompting the formation of new
sovereign independent states.

A widespread call for independence arises generally after a period
of intensification of national awareness. But under which conditions
might the claim for independence emerge? An explanation able to
account for all cases would be an extremely complicated one. Historical, economic and socio-political factors impinge upon the ways in
which communities manifest their will. Buchanan defines secession as
'a collective action, whereby a group (whether officially recognized as
a legitimate political subunit or not) attempts to become independent
from the state that presently claims jurisdiction over it and, in doing
so, seeks to remove part of the territory from the existing state'.[7]

In his analysis Buchanan distinguishes between a wide range
of arguments that could be summarized as follows. The moral

justifications for a right to secede would include: protecting liberty, furthering diversity, liberal purity, the achievement of the specific goals for which a political union was forged, the preservation of a culture, self-defence, rectifying past injustices, and consent as a necessary condition for legitimate political authority. Economic reasons to justify secession involve escaping discriminatory redistribution and enhancing efficiency. The strategic argument refers to the inclusion of a right to secede in an agreement to form a political union, and the nationalist argument is based upon the right of self-determination for 'peoples' interpreted as equivalent to what is sometimes called the normative principle of nationalism, that is, one nation, one state.[8]

The path to independence followed by Bangladesh and the events leading to the independence of the Baltic States offer substantially different examples. Ever since Pakistan's independence from British rule in 1947, the Bengalis of East Pakistan, who constituted 54 per cent of the total population of the country, had been dominated by the Urdu-speaking minority in West Pakistan. Although the Bengalis had played a crucial part in Pakistan's struggle for independence, their subsequent exclusion from all higher positions in the civil and military bureaucracies of the new country led to growing resentment. This was reinforced by a range of discriminatory policies concerning language adopted by the West Pakistani elite, including the initial insistence that Urdu should be the only state language, even though less than 1 per cent of the Bengali population could speak it. Economic disadvantages for East Pakistan and the ruling elite's persistent refusal to accommodate Bengali demands for majority rule and greater autonomy further exacerbated tension between the two halves of the country.

The Awami League, a party based entirely in East Pakistan, won almost all the seats there in the 1970 election. Its leader announced a programme of radical devolution which was refused by political and military leaders in West Pakistan; they proclaimed a state of emergency in East Pakistan and launched a campaign of military repression there. India backed the democratically elected party calling for independence. In 1971 Pakistan was divided into two independent countries.[9]

The movement towards independence emerging in the Baltic Republics in the *glasnost* era brought about by Gorbachev had its origin in the joint petition of 23 August 1979 signed by representatives of the three Baltic Republics demanding that the USSR and the two German states declare null and void the Molotov–Ribbentrop Pact. Thus, for the first time during Soviet rule, the Baltic peoples were able publicly to rediscover their history and re-examine the reality of past and current ethnic inequalities.[10] The fall of the Berlin Wall conferred renewed strength on nationalist movements in Estonia, Latvia and Lithuania, endorsing the illegality of forced incorporation and thus the call for the reinstatement of independent statehood. In March 1990 Lithuania proclaimed the restoration of the sovereign powers of the Lithuanian state. The Estonian and Latvian soviets declared their intention to re-establish independent states in March and May 1990.[11]

Few new states have been constituted since 1945. The reluctance to acknowledge a broad 'right to self-determination of peoples' in mainstream international law has contributed to the preservation of a certain stability in the nation-state system. This is a trend which has been partially reversed to allow the creation of independent states emerging out of the collapse of the Soviet Union. The right to secession was included in the USSR's constitution and a fair number of former Soviet republics have taken advantage of it by bringing to the fore a long-neglected political concept.

The future of nations without a state in the European Union

Differing degrees of national consciousness exist among the numerous national minorities forming the European Union. Most of them are part of large states which are the official members of the Union. The idea of a 'Europe of the Regions' is cherished not only by the Catalans, who place great emphasis on the opportunities that the EU will open up for national minorities, but also by the Scots, the Basques and the Welsh among other European nations without a state seeking to fulfil their cultural and political aspirations within a new Europe. They perceive the EU as an emergent political institution into which they are entering voluntarily. Even if the minorities did not have a say in the decision of the state that rules them to join the EU, they perceive a clear possibility for them to intervene in the organization of this new entity. National minorities with a considerable nationalist consciousness resent the various ways in which their political institutions were lost in the past, while others are simply unhappy about the state's management of their business. This explains the current revival of nationalism in nations without a state in Western Europe. In many cases, they show open, forward-looking attitudes, while, as Morris argues, trying to translate traditional cultural forms into modern media of expression.[12] They seek the economic and cultural invigoration of the nation, they link across boundaries, hold international meetings, build co-ordinating bodies such as the Assembly for a Europe of the Regions, and actively lobby European institutions, so that, at least in the EU, one may speak of a 'transnational ethnic' movement.

However, it is not at all clear how the European Union will develop and what role that nations without a state will be allowed to play. Europe is a problematic entity whose cultural and physical boundaries are not clear. Europe, Giner argues, 'is an entity which happens to constitute, for many of our citizens, the widest possible frame of reference in terms of their social identity, lying beyond locality, occupation and nation, as the ultimate source of what they have been able to learn in education, taste, ethics, belief, and public and private conduct'.[13]

In cultural terms, it can be argued that Europe shares a common civilization. This is a point defended by Aron and Galtung. Aron wrote in 1963 that 'Europe is less today than fifty years ago, not because internal frontiers stop people or ideas but because Europe as a whole no longer has external frontiers and each nation has opened a dialogue with the whole world.'[14] Giner develops a similar point. He emphasizes that Europe may be trying to unite precisely at the moment when its distinctiveness becomes more problematic than ever. Faced with growing cosmopolitanism, mass immigration from the rest of the world, the relentless spread of the culturally syncretic mass media, telecommunications, global interdependence and the globalization of social relationships, demographic and ecological imbalances, world trade and industry, and transnational social inequalities, specifically European characteristics may become even more blurred than they already are. Europe may lose much of its identity when confronted with the consequences and ramifications of its own historical dynamics, as recast, perfected or transformed by the peoples that once upon a time fell under its spell or were the direct offshoots of its relentless world expansion. The 'Europeanization' of the world, Giner concludes, has weakened the distinctiveness of Europe itself.[15]

The European Union is, in effect, an association of nation-states which, although performing some acts in common, remain viable states with divergences of interest and policy. As Baker and Kolinsky argue, the EU has not become a new focus of loyalty likely to replace the state. Indeed, in EU structures citizens look to their governments to defend national interests, rather than pushing integration forward.[16] The nation-state stands as a protagonist in the process towards European unity and will probably retain a substantial amount of power in the near future. Gellner argues that 'the unification of Europe, if it comes about, will diminish the rivalry between the great intra-European powers, in as far as any effective unification will deprive them of the capacity to act independently.'[17] In my view, it is possible to envisage tensions arising between France, Germany and the United Kingdom in trying to influence the principles and policies that should rule within the Union. There will be rivalry in the foreseeable future.

The reasons that prompted the initiation of a process of unity between a limited number of European nation-states did not include a grasp of the aspirations and claims of national minorities. Rather, it was state weakness, not strength, which forced many politicians, economic interest groups and social movements, to move in the direction of unity. In Giner's view, the shared plight of relative national smallness, loss of competitiveness against external powers, military weakness, the Soviet threat in the decades after the Second World War, and other similarly powerful factors, managed to weaken the seemingly inexhaustible moral and political resources of the defenders of the nation-state.[18]

The future shape of the EU has not yet been decided and the prospective role of nations without a state completely depends on it. Only a European Union of a federal type, as advocated in the European Parliament's resolution of 14 March 1990, where the principle of subsidiarity is applied, could generate a 'Europe of the Regions'. A decentralized, federal, democratic Europe would not only respond to sound economic arguments, but would also offer an adequate framework within which nations without a state could preserve and develop their culture. At present the degree of autonomy, co-operation and subsidiarity that will constitute the EU remains uncertain. It is important to consider that nation-states are the agents designing the shape and limits of an institution, the EU, that will inevitably not eliminate but radically recast their nature.

An EU based upon subsidiarity implies that nothing should be done at a higher level which can be done more effectively at a lower level. Government and services to the citizen should be controlled and administered as near the point of delivery as possible. Within this framework, the concept of a 'Europe of the Regions', as Martin argues, 'holds out the exciting possibility of reinvigorating local democracy and bringing discussion and decision-making much closer to the people'.[19] A federal Europe should ensure democratic scrutiny and accountability, avoiding the danger of transforming itself into an enormous and complicated bureaucratic institution.

Nationalism has proved a useful device in the construction of nation-states. It is also invoked by minorities which claim cultural difference and the right to autonomy. In the near future nationalism will be required to contribute to the creation of a united Europe. The economic and political intertwining of the European states has not yet developed a sense of common identity. As Aron argues, consciousness of the nation remains infinitely stronger than a sense of Europe. In his view, 'the old nations will live in the hearts of men, and love of the European nation is not yet born – assuming that it ever will be.'[20] Aron wrote this thirty years ago and his statement remains true. However, something has changed. The socio-political unity of Europe is today a project to which all member states are committed.

The construction of Europe requires the development of a 'European national consciousness', a European identity that will confer cohesion on a highly diversified but economically and politically united entity. Sociology lacks an adequate terminology to tackle the emergent Europe since it will no longer be possible to equate society and nation-state. The engineers of the new Europe will have to look at 'common European trends' and design a myth of origin, rewrite history, invent traditions, rituals and symbols that will create a new identity. But, even more important, they will have to discover a common goal, a project capable of mobilizing the energy of European citizens. They will need a common task if solidarity is to be developed among them. Nationalism will probably be invoked and once again it is not clear how it will be articulated. A future European nationalism might turn into aggressive xenophobia against immigrants escaping misery in Africa, Asia and Eastern Europe, and be concerned about the defence of a 'fortress Europe' jealous of its own prosperity. The creation of a European identity will not erase national or regional identities. Rather, it will generate concentric circles of identity, each of them invoked at different times.

6
States without a Nation

The idea of a state without a nation, or what is sometimes referred to as a 'state-nation', applies to a situation in which a state is arbitrarily designed ignoring the cultural and linguistic identities of the groups falling within its boundaries. A state-nation involves the creation of a state apparatus which controls the legitimate use of the means of violence within its territory, holds internal and external sovereignty, and receives international recognition of its status.

In Europe the emergence of states responded to the outcome of wars, annexations and pacts. In most cases an ethnic group managed to impose its language and culture on an initially divided population. Homogenization came to be perceived as a condition for the stability of the state. The political link between citizens and institutions benefited from the development of a nationalist ideology that infused a sense of forming a single community distinct from others. Confrontations with exterior powers and internal problems both contributed to the establishment of a national identity aiming at the consolidation of emergent nation-states. However, the multiethnic character of most European nation-states accounts for the unsuccessful or incomplete homogenization achieved by the state and the greater resilience of some national minorities in opposing assimilation.

It could be argued that 'states without a nation' also exist in Europe and elsewhere, since most nation-states contain more than one nation or parts of nations and some of them find it hard to establish a core of cultural, historical and linguistic elements to justify their existence. But to apply the term 'state-nation' to a Western European country would not be accurate, since in this case the problem is not the lack of a nation legitimizing the state but the existence of other nations lacking political representation and feeling alien to the state containing them. In Spain, Castilian culture and language have dominated the state since the eighteenth century and have attempted the assimilation of Catalans, Basques and Galicians. The English language and culture have prevailed within Britain. The Scots, Welsh and Cornish have been anglicized despite the current re-emergence of nationalism in these areas.

The notion of state without a nation perfectly applies to Third World countries where in most cases there is no sense in which a nation precedes the emergence of the state. This chapter focuses upon the development of nationalism in the Third World once it had been exported from Europe to Asia and Africa. It studies the differences arising between initial forms of nationalism as a movement directed against colonialism and engaged in the struggle for independence, and nationalism's subsequent transformation into a political discourse employed by new leaders in their attempt to construct a nation capable of sustaining the legitimacy of the state they inherited from the colonial era. The text is primarily concerned with African states south of the Sahara, although it draws parallels with some South Asian countries.

The state in Third World countries

The impact of industrial techniques upon warfare and communications favoured the relatively quick processes by means of which the leading European powers conquered the lands of the so-called Third World in the nineteenth and early twentieth centuries. The kingdoms and empires existing in most parts of these areas were defeated and, in many cases, destroyed. New states – called colonies or protectorates – were formed in their place. The colonial authorities named the new states, drew their borders, built up their capital cities, and established a central administration and political institutions to suit their economic needs and prestige. As a result, each colony was 'a collection of peoples and old states, or fragments of these, brought together within the same boundaries'.[1]

Each such territory came to include a mosaic of different ethnic communities and tribes. Polyethnic state-based territorialisms became the norm in Africa and South Asia. As Smith argues, 'they alone confer legitimacy on states which possess no other basis, whether it be in popular assent or cultural community. African states today derive their legitimacy largely from the circumstances of their origins in deliberate acts of creation – by aliens for alien purposes – and in the resulting location they enjoy.'[2] States in Asia and Africa are both 'heirs to, and beneficiaries of, the European imperial order'.[3] The artificial and imposed character of the state in such territories accounts for most of the troubles in which they found themselves submerged after obtaining independence. Probably the major problem faced by these twentieth-century states is their fragility. The newly created states initiated a struggle to replace pre-national ties with feelings of national identity and loyalty. Concepts of internal sovereignty and citizenship exported from the West needed to be assimilated by a multiethnic population which, in most cases, was illiterate. The task of the state was enormous. Often, to protect its fragile character, the state favoured a centralized administration, placed a strong emphasis upon the inviolability of its territorial *status quo* and stressed the need for political order while employing varying degrees of coercion.

The expansion of the nation-state structure to Third World countries meant their inclusion as independent actors within the nation-state system. Sixty-six countries attained independence from colonial rule between 1945 and 1968. However, the euphoria accompanying the celebration of freedom soon turned sour. Independence has been mostly anticlimactic. The reasons for this stem from the incapacity of the new states to eliminate economic backwardness and the difficulty of creating a coherent civil society out of a population as profoundly heterogeneous in itself as in relation to the state.

Once independence was achieved, the state needed economic success to gain approval. For the majority of new states, Mayall argues, economic development was not just a technical question; it was the only strategy available to governments which at once was undeniably modern – and therefore legitimate by virtue of this fact – and seemed to offer a means of detaching loyalties from clan, tribe and region and transferring them to the new state.[4] However, the state was unable to fulfil the expectations of those who envisaged immediate economic development and the expansion of welfare amongst a population willing to begin a new existence free from colonial rulers. Thus, many post-colonial states seeking legitimacy from the pursuit of economic development could no longer sustain such claims and often turned towards the economic superpowers. By 1945 the United States and the Soviet Union were competing for the attention of the Third World. Capitalism and Marxism-Leninism took as a common objective the industrialization of society – a feature to which it was rarely perceived there was any alternative. Industrialization was presented as the major feature accompanying modernity, as 'an imperative and prerequisite for modern statehood, whose absence was both a challenge and a shame'.[5]

However, for Africa and the majority of Third World countries in Asia, entering the Western world involved becoming dependent. In Badie's and Birnbaum's words, 'the state in Africa and Asia is a purely imported product, a pale imitation of the diametrically opposite European political and social systems, a foreign body which is moreover overweight, inefficient and a source of violence.'[6] Bayart agrees and concludes that the drafting of the state in Africa has been a failure, since 'the single party, the military regime, the presumed charismatic authority of the presumed "African" chief, become the modern counterparts to the despotism of the "bloodthirsty petty kings" against which the civilizing mission of colonialism fought.'[7] An exception to this pattern of economic failure is the recent economic success of some South Asian countries which have turned to capitalism.

Historical, social, political and economic circumstances leading to the establishment of the nation-state in Asia and Africa have no parallel with the context within which the nation-state emerged in Western Europe. In the former, the dichotomy between tradition and modernity (industrialization and Western life-style and values) leads to a series of gaps developing between the diverse groups integrated within the state. The absence of a coherent civil society proves one of the greatest obstacles in guaranteeing the stability of the nation-state. The distance between the formation of the state apparatus and a usually deprived population trapped by powerful ethnic ties and traditional forms of life illustrates the distance existing amongst the citizens of the same state. The economic backwardness and the profoundly heterogeneous nature of most states in Asia and Africa account for their failure to integrate the diverse ethnic groups and tribes into a citizenship-centered national structure.

Nationalism and the struggle for independence

In Africa, previous to the emergence of nationalism, there existed what Smith terms 'primary resistance' and 'millennial' movements.[8] The former lacked the central concept of the 'nation' and were basically set up to oppose and resist European domination. The latter 'often acted as an unconscious conduit for the dissemination of pan-Negro ideas and a sense of African dignity and "redemption" which fed the stream of Pan-African sentiments and helped to train a new generation of African religious leaders imbued with the ideas of Black consciousness'.[9]

African millennial movements denounced European penetration and contributed to the growth of nationalist feelings, despite lacking a secular ideology and a concept of the 'nation'. Separatist churches such as Sundkler's 'Ethiopian Churches' promoted the rise of African nationalism in an indirect and unintended way.

The greatest impetus to the development of a nationalism seeking the independence of African states was prompted by the events surrounding the Second World War (1939–45). The colonial powers mobilized large human and material resources from the African soil in their struggle against Nazism. The Allies were engaged in a war which had the exclusion of certain groups – Jews, Gypsies, Communists – as a priority. Ideas about racial purity brought into being genocidal policies implemented above all by Hitler's regime. The fight against such forms of discrimination prompted the Allied powers to promise in the Atlantic Charter that after the war they would ensure that every nation, large or small, would enjoy the right to self-determination. Akintoye points out that though this promise was meant for European countries only, emergent nationalist leaders in Africa chose to believe that their countries would also benefit from the new policy and gain the right to rule themselves.[10]

The dangers, fears and anxieties shared by whites and blacks in the battlefield made vulnerable the old image of 'white superiority'. Africans fighting abroad widened their horizons and developed a sense of equality with whites. Sithole emphasizes the key role played by the United Nations in the emancipation of Africa. He writes:

> Just imagine the impact on millions of people who had been taught and told for many decades that they were not fit to rule themselves; that they had been created to be ruled by the white race only; that their place under the sun was second- or third-class citizenship in the land of their birth; that they were only equals among themselves but not with any people outside their own; and that their chief function was to draw water and hew wood for foreigners who ruled them. And then an international organization reverses the whole trend by telling them they were equals of everyone else, and were entitled to self-government, freedom, and independence, and to first-class citizenship; and that they existed to further their own ends not those of others.[11]

The 1945 UN Charter made a basic contribution to the proliferation of nationalist movements in Asia and Africa by recognizing the right of all peoples to self-determination. The fifth Pan-African Congress in 1945 in Manchester affirmed 'the right of all people to control their own destiny'. The demand for autonomy and independence for black Africa represented a radical shift from previous meetings in which independence was never addressed as a real possibility.[12]

During the 1920s the growth of national awareness in Africa received significant influence from black Americans fighting against oppression and racial discrimination in the United States. Black people in the United States showed great concern about the situation of Africans under colonialism. By the middle of the 1930s, nationalist organizations such as the Tanganyika African Association were beginning to emerge, but large-scale nationalist parties did not come into being until the aftermath of the Second World War. Freedom from colonial rulers and independence for territorial units lacking cultural homogeneity but administratively organized to form a state were the outcome of the initial nationalist movements.

At that time nationalism received further stimulus from a small number of African people educated according to Western standards. These incipient elites drew mainly on English and French democratic nationalist conceptions. They were Westernized and soon formed new groups opposing the old rural chiefs and colonial castes.[13] The expansion of Christianity also contributed to the dissemination of ideas about social equality and solidarity which could be invoked by the new leaders. The new religion became a major opponent of the continuity of traditional cults and ethnic religions which in some cases were relegated to a secondary position. However, the acceptance of Western ideas and values did not count when the well-prepared African elites attempted to break the colonizers' monopoly of power. The African intelligentsia was denied access to political and economic positions. To give an example, in the Gold Coast in 1949 only some 14 per cent of the top civil posts were held by Africans.[14] A similar situation occurred in India where British rule required the willing collaboration of an Indian establishment. Macaulay's Minute on Education of 1835 saw the answer in the creation of a social stratum of British Indians: 'a class of persons, Indian in blood and colour, but English in taste, in opinions, in morals and in intellect'.[15] Yet in the long term this became a source of conflict: the British-Indians were rejected by the Indians and could not fulfil their expectations within the British establishment. They were as qualified as the British but suffered automatic exclusion from top posts.

The African elites as well as the Indian ones resented the way in which they were treated; they felt excluded from the decision-making processes that decided their country's future. The exclusion suffered by African elites pushed them towards nationalism as a discourse capable of legitimizing their right to control their land's own affairs.

A further significant element contributing to the spread of pro-independence ideas in Africa was the growth of an African press which became popular in the new urban areas created by colonialism. As Anderson argues, newspapers perform a crucial role in the construction of the boundaries of one's own country.[16] Africans imagined their community as a territorial political entity. African-owned newspapers were to be found in both British and French West Africa. Most African newspapers were short-lived, but amongst those which enjoyed a longer life and exerted considerable influence are the *Lagos Weekly Record*, the *Gold Coast Independent* and the *Sierra Leone Weekly News*.[17]

Three basic features can be discerned when analysing African nationalism in the period 1945–60: the territorial character of the new states, the acceptance of democracy as a political idea informing the emergent states, and the development of pan-Africanism.[18] The territorial foundation of African countries implied the acceptance of the arbitrary colonial partition of the African land. Nationalist parties, far from seeking to dismantle the state and draw new boundaries, decided to fight colonialism while retaining the territorial divisions imposed by the West. The international recognition of these boundaries would have made it extremely difficult for ethnic groups contained within these states to set up successful pro-independence movements. Ethnic or secessionist self-determination, as Neuberger argues, is widely condemned by the political establishment of Africa – the Organization of African Unity and the majority of the ruling governments. Such ethnic secessionist movements frequently involved a *Kulturnation* (e.g. the Somalis in the Ogaden) or a territory with at least one ethno-cultural core (e.g. the Ibos in Biafra). In fact, 'anti-colonial self-determination is indeed hardly national self-determination as it is colony-based and not nation-based.'[19]

African anti-colonial nationalism in the 1940s and 1950s was national in the sense that it was directed against foreign European rule, and pleaded for democratic self-determination as embedded in the liberal democratic tradition. Independence brought a change of rulers but left untouched the values and structure of a centralized bureaucratic state that in many cases appealed to coercion and even violence to impose its supremacy upon an extremely divided population. Independence liberated ethnic nationalisms within the emergent state nationalisms, and in some cases – Nigeria, India, Malaysia, Indonesia,

Pakistan – threatened the anti-colonial nationalism whose objective was the conservation of the state and the replacement of the colonial rulers. In India, nationalist movements of Muslims calling for an independent Pakistan, some Bengalis for an independent Bengal, and some Sikhs for an independent Sikh state challenged the integrity of the Indian state. Class, caste, locality, ethnic origin, religion and language formed separate layers of identity that added to the complexity of creating a single nation out of an inherited, arbitrarily designed state.

The requirement of dealing with a multiethnic state encouraged many African and Asian states to pursue a policy of strict control to ensure the state's unity. Where ethnic cleavages cut across class boundaries, Smith points out, they may mute incipient class conflict. When ethnic groups are also aligned along class lines and feel discriminated against they form a potential focus for ethnic revolt.[20]

By the 1960s and 1970s the scarcity of resources, a backward economy, demographic pressures and constant ethnic conflict forced many African countries to abandon the liberal democratic policies announced prior to and immediately after independence. Neuberger stresses that 'only very rarely in post-colonial Africa were the linkages between democracy and nationalism and between human rights and independence re-established.'[21] Yet, while states achieving independence in the 1960s experimented with democracy for a brief period, those that became independent in the 1970s frequently perceived national self-determination as an opportunity to form a national government that was not democratic.

Sithole defines pan-Africanism as 'a common identification of the peoples of African descent who have discovered their common destiny and who demand to be treated as equals of men (individuals) of other races'.[22] Pan-Africanism emerged as a reaction against the doctrine of racial inferiority existing at the core of colonialism. The common experience of colonialism was employed as a unifying factor amongst the peoples of Africa. Smith argues that 'by utilizing race-consciousness for unifying ends, it was hoped to counteract the incipient ethnic separatism, and the even greater risk and fear of such movements.'[23] Pan-Africanism reflected the Africans' solidarity in their struggle for the eradication of white oppression; it also played a key part in linking up nationalist leaders in several African territories with their West Indian and American black counterparts. After years of degradation and slavery, pan-Africanism fixed the basis for moral regeneration by encouraging the protection and dissemination of an originally pan-African culture which contributed to the development of an 'us' identity based upon the discovery of black dignity.

However, the achievements of the Organization of African Unity (OAU) have been modest since very few African countries are ready to surrender their recently won sovereignty for the sake of the creation of a single African nation. Sharp disagreements amongst African leaders echo the different meanings attributed to the expression 'African unity'.

Nationalism after independence

Nationalists had a well-defined objective in colonial Africa: freedom from European domination and independence for their country. Such a message succeeded in spreading a sense of solidarity amongst an otherwise diverse population now united to pursue a common end and fight a common enemy. Once independence was achieved, the new leaders felt overwhelmed by enormous problems ranging from the need to preserve – and in most countries create – national unity, to the fulfilment of the economic expectations of their peoples. A programme of social and economic measures aimed at the economic transformation of the new states became an imperative for the new regimes. Thus political concerns shifted from constitutional to economic issues.

Only a number of Africans were ready to assume power in the now independent Western-style states. The colonial years had offered limited opportunities to indigenous peoples. Racial and cultural prejudice played a large part in restricting the number of recruits to central colonial services; Africans were not admitted into senior posts in the army or the civil service until almost the end of the colonial era. An African bourgeoisie did not materialize until the 1960s.

The African leaders defended the integrity of the state and turned to pan-Africanism in an attempt to nullify the cultural and psychological effects of colonial prejudice and discrimination. They acted as 'managers of modernization' by channelling and refracting Western influences.[24]

The socio-political environment previous to independence contributed to the elevation of some leaders to the category of 'prophet-liberators' (Gandhi, Nehru, Sukarno, Nkrumah, Mohammed V, Ben Bella, Keita, Azikiwe, Nasser, Bandaranaike).[25] Yet the vast gap between the Western-educated elites and the bulk of a mostly illiterate population increased after independence. The quasi-religious character of some leaders was debilitated; they could not fulfil their promises. An immediate improvement in the quality of life of the masses proved to be beyond their power. Furthermore, in most cases the new leaders did not change the structure of the state and retained the colonizer's privileges. The fragility of their government and institutions led to an increasing hostility against all sorts of opposition to political parties as well as movements seeking the independence of ethnic minorities within established states. Independence brought civil war to Sudan, Zaire, Chad and Nigeria. Kenya, Ghana and Zambia witnessed inter-ethnic rivalries and antagonisms that threatened the integrity of the state.

Ethnic conflict came to the fore in countries such as Nigeria and Kenya because certain ethnic groups had produced more highly educated individuals than others, or formed a large part of the population and thus commanded more political power. Fears of the domination of some ethnic groups by others resembled the Western European nation-state pattern in countries such as Spain or Britain, where one group has tended to dominate the state apparatus: the Castilians in the former, the English in the latter.

The rulers of independent African countries had also to deal with pre-colonial institutions – the kings and chiefs. In most of the former French colonies such institutions were weak; however, in a large number of British colonies the status of traditional sources of power commanded considerable respect. The leaders only rarely formed any sort of partnership with the old chiefs (Sierra Leone, Nigeria); in most cases they showed a strong determination to defend their status and that of the institutions they had inherited from the Europeans. But the anticlimactic character of independence, and the failure to develop an 'integral state' from a 'soft state',[26] led some prominent sectors of these populations to revitalize their ethnic identities and loyalties.

The major task confronted by nationalist intellectuals and rulers after independence was to create a nation to legitimize the state. They launched a revolution 'as much cultural, even epistemological, as it was political . . . they attempted to transform the symbolic framework through which people experienced social reality, and thus, to the extent that life is what we make of it all, that reality itself.'[27] The nationalist discourse had to generate a collective subject to which, in Geertz's view, 'the actions of the state could be internally connected in creating or trying to create, an experimental "we" from whose will the activities of government seem spontaneously to flow'.[28] A common national identity containing the myths and symbols around which the people could be united was required to confer significance on the activities of the state and by extension on the civil life of its citizens.

As Geertz argues, 'the transfer of sovereignty from a colonial regime to an independent one is more than a mere shift of power from foreign hands to native ones; it is a transformation of the whole pattern of political life, a metamorphosis of subjects into citizens.'[29]

Nations took shape on the basis of political, rather than ethnic, communities. The leaders engaged in what have been termed 'nation-building' processes and ventured upon integration through the diffusion of a common culture. National integration involved the assimilation of ethnic groups into a single homogeneous language and culture system. In Sudan four million out of seven and a half million people in the North claimed Arab ethnic origin, representing 39 per cent of the entire population of Sudan; in the Southern provinces only six thousand out of a population of nearly three million claimed Arabic as their native language. Once the nationalists took power, they set in motion a programme for national integration based upon the expansion of Islam and the Arabic language.[30] In Ethiopia the state took the initiative in imposing Christianity on the people. The traditional method of promoting conversion among unbelievers was to deny them land-holding rights and state office. Under Haile Selassie the expansion of the Church was financed by public funds. In the 1950s leaders of Muslim communities in Ethiopia believed they represented over one half of the population. However, the unwillingness of the state to carry out a census made it impossible to prove the validity of these figures. The imperial regime ignored Islam and discriminated against the public use of Arabic.[31] Sri Lanka (formerly Ceylon) gained independence from British rule in 1948. Two major languages, Sinhalese and Tamil, were spoken in the island: the former was the mother tongue of 11 million people practising Buddhism; the latter was spoken by 5 million people of mixed religious and ethnic groups.[32] After independence, linguistic and religious distinctions were used as a pretext to create exclusive secular and political groups competing for advantage and power. In 1956 Sinhalese was declared the sole official language in Ceylon. This represented an indirect attack upon the affluent Tamil middle classes. In 1959, when Banderanaike attempted a compromise on the language issue, he was assassinated by a Buddhist monk.[33]

Common culture and language are not the only elements activated in the construction of a nation. To develop a common consciousness, a consciousness of forming a group, the citizens of the state lay out a common political project concerning their future and usually attempt to strengthen it by emphasizing past memories and experiences. Nationalism invokes a common past and selects and reinterprets certain events to increase a sense of coherence amongst the members of a given group. Past, present and future are fused to bestow on the community a sense of continuity upon which the transcendent character of the nation is founded. The limited overlap between the new states and the pre-colonial political units poses a serious dilemma for African intellectuals. The need for nationhood involves a need for history, for continuity and depth, for heroes and myths, and for a final refutation of the colonial legend that Africa has no history. But the rediscovery of history 'can rarely serve to strengthen the present state-nation, for history is to a large extent fragmented and ethnic and contains many conflicts and wars between groups which now find themselves in the same state'.[34] The key issue here is that there is little pre-colonial history which could be selected to defend the present *status quo* and very few genuinely indigenous political traditions to draw on. This contributes to the difficulties in overcoming the intrinsic fragility of artificially created states founded upon a heterogeneous population.

The colonial rulers instrumentalized existing tribal-ethnic and religious divisions in society through a policy of divide and rule. Bayart argues that 'most situations where the structuring of the contemporary political arena seems to be enunciated in terms of ethnicity relate to identities which did not exist a century ago, or, at least, were then not as clearly defined.'[35] In his view, the concept of the ethnic group was one of the ideological premises of the colonial administration and has become 'the means of affirming one's own existence and hence the language of relationships between the subject peoples themselves'.[36] The colonial bureaucracy and the missionaries, particularly the Protestants who helped in the standardization and extension of regional languages through education and the translation of the Bible, contributed to the extension of ethnic consciousness.

After the 1857–58 Mutiny, the British Raj came to choose religion as a key all-India principle of division between Muslims and Hindus. Harris stresses that

> up to this time, 'India' did not exist for the overwhelming majority of the inhabitants. It was a geographical not a political social or cultural concept. Those who espoused the complex customs grouped under the terms Islam and Hinduism did not constitute groups (other than in the pure classification sense). Neither had a sense of identity (or, insofar as they did, it was local or dynastic, not all-Indian) nor did they constitute a social or political community. Nor was the Mutiny self-evidently Muslim.[37]

However, by the end of the nineteenth century the British imposition of a fictional religious basis for India was becoming real and evoking a new Indian fiction of Hinduism which would, in time, also become real.[38]

The nation-states of the Third World did not come into being as a result of processes of social change similar or comparable to those which shaped the European nation-state system. The simultaneity of old tribes and externally imposed states can only be understood within this historical concept.[39] Post-colonial conflicts are primarily based upon struggles for resources. Ethnicity today is perceived as a channel through which competition for the acquisition of wealth, power or status is expressed. As Tibi puts it, 'the ethnicization of conflict' suggests that tribalism has been revived under a new cover and that it obstructs the process of creation of a single national identity able to replace old loyalties.[40]

7
Globalization, Modernity and National Identity

One of the major features of the current era is the strengthening of globalizing processes. I understand globalization to mean 'the intensification of worldwide social relations which link distant localities in such a way that local happenings are shaped by events occurring miles away and vice versa'.[1] Space and time are redefined. The perceptions of the physical limits of space are altered. The time required to produce and process information has been reduced to such an extent that we can already perceive a dramatic gap between that and other human time experiences. Globalization implies the possibility of referring to 'human society', something that has never existed before, in the sense that now all the possible actors are on stage at once.

Globalization can be addressed from three main perspectives. The first is the global character of the nation-state system in so far as the political arena is based upon a division into sovereign unities that rule within clearly demarcated territories and have the capability of acting at a supranational level. In this respect the nation-state has become the political actor *par excellence* on a global scale. The second is the role of capitalism as a fundamental globalizing influence that touches upon the economic order. The so-called 'world-system theory', of which Wallerstein is the main advocate, presents a picture of the modern world as divided into core, semi-periphery and periphery.[2] The main shortcoming of Wallerstein's approach is his insistence upon the role of capitalism as the single dominant institutional nexus, responsible for modern transformations. The third is the creation of a global scientific community within which a constant flow of information allows a rapid diffusion of ideas.

However, the meaning of globalization is not exhausted by the recognition of these three areas in which it takes place. Globalization also implies an awareness that the whole of humanity has to face a set of common problems that cannot be solved individually. Global problems require global solutions, and our world needs to find new ways of confronting fundamental questions that challenge the future of humanity. Modern societies rely heavily upon a continual flow of information that increases the artificial or constructed characteristics of social life. People know about the risk of a nuclear disaster, the increasing degradation of the planet as a result of a continuous exploitation of natural resources, the inequality between First and Third World countries. All these factors emphasize the globalization of human interdependencies to such a degree that modern societies are the first in history to have the possibility of finally exterminating themselves, but also, and more importantly, of creating a new world shaped by the decisions of people living within it. Globalization adds a significant new dimension to the life of individuals in so far as it widens their horizon and opens up new perspectives to the consequences of their actions.

Intrinsic to globalization is the dialectic of the local and the global, a process by which local events are transformed and shaped under the influence of the extension of social connections stretching across time and space. At the same time, local happenings achieve a completely new significance when they are removed from the perceived time and space where they take place. The local and the global intertwine forming a web in which both elements are transformed as a result of their own interconnections. Globalization expresses itself through the tension between the forces of the global community and those of cultural particularity, ethnic and cultural fragmentation, and homogenization.

This chapter studies the connection between globalization, modernity and nationalism. In so doing, it explores the possibilities for the emergence of a 'global identity' and discusses the different reactions to globalization processes stemming from a 'local' level. The renewed strength and appeal of 'national identity' and nationalism stand as a secular response to the quest for identity in a world threatened by increasing homogenization. A further element that will be taken into account when analysing the consequences of and responses to globalization is the unexpected success of Islamic Fundamentalism as a radical movement opposing modernity and secularization.

Globalization and culture

Members of a culture usually share some kind of self-awareness and a sense of boundaries. Each culture is located in a particular space and time. The intensity and rapidity of today's global cultural flow transforms the world into a singular place where processes of cultural integration and disintegration take place. The extension of global cultural interrelatedness leads to persistent cultural interaction and exchange which produce both cultural homogeneity and cultural disorder. Appadurai distinguishes five dimensions of global culture: ethnoscapes, by which he means the flow of people (immigrants, tourists, refugees, exiles and guest workers); technoscapes, which refer to the flow of machinery produced by multinational and national corporations and government agencies; finanscapes, which are rapid flows of money in the currency markets and stock exchanges; mediascapes, the flow of images and information produced and distributed by newspapers, magazines, television, films; and ideoscapes, linked to flows of images associated with state or counter-state ideologies which comprise elements of the Western Enlightenment world-view – images of democracy, freedom, welfare, rights, etc.[3] However, practical problems arise from intercultural communication that can lead to either an increasing tolerance or intolerance towards difference. Cross-cultural comparison, competition and the possibility of intercultural misunderstandings are examples.

A crucial question when dealing with the impact of globalization upon culture is whether we are moving towards a unitary global culture or, on the contrary, whether globalization will strengthen the power and favour the blossoming of particular cultures. Globalization when applied to culture is an enabling as well as a constraining phenomenon. By enabling, I mean the unprecedented possibilities for expansion and reproduction of particular cultures that the development of new technologies has favoured. The constraining aspect refers to the undeniable difference in access to resources between different cultures. While some traits and symbols of particular cultures are known worldwide, others fall into oblivion and are ignored. Why are certain elements of alien cultures incorporated into the lives of individuals and assimilated, while others are 'mummified' and presented as museum pieces instead of being absorbed and integrated? These questions inevitably lead to a fact that cannot be ignored: that is, the relation between the role of a culture and the particular position of power that the nation to which this culture belongs occupies within the world system.

I want to suggest that, although as a consequence of globalization cultures tend to overlap and mingle, we are witnessing a process by which only very few cultures can be elevated to the category of 'global cultures', while most cultures find themselves enmeshed in a global struggle for their self-determination. As Tenbruck puts it: 'in contrast to earlier epochs where only a few cultures clashed at their geographic borders, modern developments through their universal presence and penetration now bring all cultures into a network of interrelationships.'[4]

The present revival of ethnicity responds to a need for identity, but an identity of a local, rather than a global, character. The creation of a global identity presents several major problems that derive from the impossibility of fulfilling two vital conditions for success: continuity over time and differentiation from others. The former is the case because, while national identity relies heavily upon a common past as a means to create solidarity, global identity has no common memories to invoke in order to summon up the consciousness of forming a group. The nation as a space within which culture is produced and transmitted is not an eternal entity, but has deep roots in the pre-modern era. I have argued in discussing the origin of nations that cultures are historically constructed as a response to the needs and desires of particular communities. Cultures interpret the world and create meaning, thus providing individuals with a sense of identity. They are the outcome of long processes stretching across generations and are based upon a set of selected shared memories which permit the imagining of the community as a transcendent entity.

A 'global identity' should aim at the creation of a sense of community amongst all peoples. This poses fundamental and so far unsolvable questions. First, how to construct a sense of continuity without a common past? There are no common memories. Rather, the cultures which will enter and build up a potential 'global identity' possess separate and often mutually antagonistic histories. Second, what language should be adopted as a 'global' language? A common identity requires the possibility of communicating with other members of the community, and although English, Spanish and Chinese may claim to be spoken by millions of people, there is no globally shared language. It could be argued that among certain elites English is becoming a *lingua franca*, but a 'global identity' has to involve ordinary people, it requires a popular base. The great success of nationalism stems from its capacity to appeal to a socially and politically diversified population and mobilize them. The concept of a 'global identity' seems far removed from acquiring such capacity and stands as a soft alternative to the passionately felt national identities.

On the other hand, difference from others can only be achieved when there are 'others', and the hypothesis of a 'global identity' implies to some extent the denial or replacement of single identities. One of the more striking consequences of globalization is the suddenly multiplied awareness of the existence of 'others'. This does not mean that we understand them better, but simply that otherness has now been extended to 'distant strangers', some of them so remote that they cannot even be portrayed as the 'other' whom our identity is based upon or constructed against. They do now seem familiar, we recognize their faces, but they mostly belong to the world as we see it on our television screens, and in films and newspapers. They are somewhat artificially created others who do not interact with us. National identities emphasize the differences between otherwise relatively similar groups. In many cases national identity focuses upon minimal differences with neighbouring communities.[5] In any case, the genesis of a sense of community and the unfolding of solidarity amongst the peoples of the world are necessary components of the eventual emergence of a 'global identity'. So far, they both seem to lie beyond the bounds of possibility.

Globalization and national identity

I have referred to the dialectic of the local and the global as an intrinsic aspect of globalization. Yet local transformations are part and parcel of globalization. At the heart of modern societies lies a rapid multiplication of contacts and a constant flow of messages; both elements destroy the homogeneity of individual cultures. Globalization is pervasive and nobody can escape its consequences. So far, I have studied the implications of globalization on one side of the local–global dialectic. I shall now move on to analyse the local transformations that form the other pole of globalization.

The current revival of nationalism lies at the core of local transformations. In my view, the present renewed emphasis upon national identity springs from the need for collective as well as individual identity. According to Melucci, the highly differentiated relations typical of complex societies are unable to provide forms of membership and identification to meet individuals' needs for self-realization, communicative interaction and recognition. He stresses that the bureaucratic and impersonal nature of complex organizations makes them ill-suited to achieving these goals.[6] Nationalism, I argue, appears as a reaction to two intrinsic constituents of modernity that are closely linked to globalization: radical doubt and fragmentation. In conditions of modernity, and as a result of the possibility of interaction between entirely different cultures and intense and continuous changes, we have reached a point at which nothing can be taken for granted. All decisions have to be discussed and are the fruit of choices at an international and national, as well as at a personal level. Weber's statement: 'it can never be the task of an empirical science to provide binding norms and ideals from which directives for immediate practical activity can be derived',[7] is now being applied to all areas of knowledge and aspects of social life.

In a world of doubt and fragmentation, tradition acquires new importance. It appears as 'an intrinsically meaningful routine'[8] that stems from the common past of a concrete community. Nationalism relies heavily upon tradition in so far as it has common memories as one of its central features. But not only common memories are important, 'common amnesia' is also crucial, since tradition is constructed by the careful selection of events which are portrayed as key elements in the history of the community. It could also be argued that, whenever necessary, tradition may be, and often is, invented. But in emphasizing the role of tradition and its capacity to give meaning, something urgently needed in a world that accepts uncertainty as one of its primary elements, I do not wish to imply that the current re-emergence of nationalism necessarily involves the revival of conservatism. To do so would be to ignore a further and crucial dimension of nationalism: that is, its proposal of a common future in which the nation should be renewed and regenerated.

Nationalism entails cultural resistance, and challenges modern societies by vindicating what I shall call 'identity politics', that is, the claim for cultural difference based upon ethnicity. I consider it crucially important that the nationalisms which are currently showing renewed strength and energy are primarily those which stem from nations without a state. Identity politics involves a progressive element, and the nationalist movements that represent it stand alongside the peace, ecological or feminist movements in so far as they stand for the different, the powerless. They constitute a voice which can no longer be ignored in a world that claims to accept democracy as the prime legitimizing element. When goals and means have to be negotiated and society constructed, all voices need to be taken into account. Globalization, as I have mentioned above, has both enabling and constraining capacities. It constrains national identities by breaking their cultural homogeneity. But at the same time, its enabling capacity not only offers individual cultures the possibility of using new technologies to reproduce themselves, but also opens new channels by which these same cultures can claim the right to survive, develop and flourish.

My approach to the relation between globalization and national identity demands a brief discussion of the role played by individuals and their particular need for identity in conditions of modernity. Modern societies produce some kind of ontological insecurity as a consequence of the uncertainty and fragmentation that lie at their core. Yet, as Laing describes it, an ontologically insecure individual feels 'precariously differentiated from the rest of the world, so that his identity and autonomy are always in question. He may lack the experience of his own temporal continuity. He may not possess an over-riding sense of personal consistency or cohesiveness.'[9] Ontological insecurity generates anxiety and jeopardizes the individual's capacity to relate to others. Laing distinguishes three forms of anxiety: engulfment, implosion and petrification.[10] I shall focus upon engulfment as I consider it to be of particular relevance to my purposes here. In a situation of engulfment, the individual 'dreads relatedness as such, with anyone or anything or, indeed, even with him, because his uncertainty about the stability of his autonomy lays him open to the dread lest in any relationship he will lose his autonomy and identity'.[11]

The main manoeuvre used to preserve identity is isolation. Modern cultures cannot afford isolation: globalization stretches interconnections and makes cultures aware of interdependencies, whilst at the same time it creates them. The danger of engulfment is evident to individuals who witness how some cultures become more globalized than others, and also see the threat of homogenization as its consequence. Isolation is no longer possible. Thus, single cultures face the threat of loss of being through absorption into other cultures which possess greater means to reproduce and expand. Community of culture and unity of meaning are the main sources that allow the construction and experience of national identity.

Globalization and Islamic Fundamentalism

Globalization has been made possible by the unrivalled development of technology that has taken place in the last fifty years. Modernity has created the conditions of possibility for a new era in which information is produced and transmitted almost simultaneously. Globalization originated in the West and has been primarily concerned with the expansion of Western ideas, values, life-styles and technology. Two major reactions to globalization processes can be distinguished. The first, as I have shown above, points to the 'local' resistance to homogenization which produces the exacerbation of a feeling of insecurity together with a fear of losing one's own national identity. In this context, nationalism has emerged as a secular global movement which vindicates the right to be different. It affects nation-states as well as national minorities struggling for autonomy.

The second response to globalization has its roots in the Third World. Its name is Islamic Fundamentalism. Globalization enables constant interaction between remote parts of the world, but it also highlights in a repetitive way that a 'global' world is not an 'equal' world. Inequalities come to the fore constantly; they affect the allocation of resources, the distribution of wealth, military power, and the number of choices available to individuals living in different areas. To complement the picture, globalization has also uncovered the rampant *anomie* suffered by many men and women struggling to find a set of values around which they can organize their lives. The secular and rational legacy of the Enlightenment does not seem capable of providing satisfactory answers to daily problems. The dream of an equal society in which individuals would be free from alienation and ready to start a happy life has sunk with the dismissal of communism prompted by the collapse of the Soviet Union.

The attempts to Westernize the Third World have been to a large extent a failure. The Western comforts once promised to former colonies never did materialize. Dependence has become more acute and probably one of the key ideas brought about by decolonization processes is the need to find an alternative to an imposed Western style which has proved ill-suited to resolving their social, political and economic troubles. The resurgence of Islam and in particular of Islamic Fundamentalism has to be regarded from this perspective. Its spectacular success springs from three main elements: (1) its competence to offer an alternative view of modernity; (2) its aptitude for providing a strong sense of identity and dignity; and (3) its use of globalization to spread its message. Fundamentalism, in Gellner's words, 'repudiates the tolerant modernist claim that the faith in question means something much milder, far less exclusive, altogether less demanding and much more accommodating; above all something quite compatible with all other faiths, even, or especially, with the lack of faith'.[12] At present, fundamentalist attitudes can be found concerning not only religion but all sorts of moral dilemmas and attitudes. Religious fundamentalism exists in many religions, but today it shows most strength in Islam. The underlying idea of religious fundamentalism, in Gellner's view, is that 'a given faith is to be upheld firmly in its full and literal form, free of compromise, softening, re-interpretation or diminution. It presupposes that the core of religion is *doctrine* rather than ritual, and also that this doctrine can be fixed with precision and finality which further presupposes *writing*.'[13]

Islamic Fundamentalism denies relativism, and at the same time refuses to establish a distinction between the religious and the political arena. Civil and political society, personal and public matters are solved by appealing to the same core values. Islam offers a radical alternative to what many consider one of the greatest achievements of the French Revolution, that is, the separation of state and church. Religious leaders are now political leaders ready to offer a clear-cut interpretation of reality and firm moral patterns to their followers. As a result we are witnessing the emergence of an extremely coherent society that shows a high level of solidarity amongst its members, which involves readiness for sacrifice and the enhancement of a sense of community.

The existence of a common enemy plays a key role in the construction of a group's identity. Islamic Fundamentalism rejects the West and turns to its own doctrine and tradition in search of an alternative to secular nationalism, socialism and capitalism. 'Dependence on Western models of development is seen as the cause of political and military failures', as Esposito points out, 'blind imitation of the West and an uncritical Westernization of Muslim societies . . . led to a cultural dependence which threatened the loss of Muslim identity.'[14] The unfolding of Islamic movements in Tunisia or Iran can be explained as a product of a growing opposition between state and society and in particular 'as a revolt against the secular modernizing state'.[15] Islamic Fundamentalism puts forward an impulse towards self-reformation and purification which, as Gellner argues, blends with reactive nationalism, making it exceedingly hard to separate the two.[16]

The cultural and religious values defended by Islamic Fundamentalism firmly regulate the daily life of its followers. They allow the restoration of a sense of identity and dignity that springs from within their own culture. The shame of backwardness, when compared with Western developed countries, is replaced by pride and the conviction that doctrine and faith can regenerate the community and redress the wrongs of millions of peoples many of whom live under conditions of poverty. The lack of alternative ideologies in the West, the painful and so far unsuccessful search for political discourses able to mobilize the masses – except for nationalism – contrast with the capacity of Islam to present itself as a reservoir of traditional values and a growing religious movement capable of making an extremely strong social and political impact.

Traditions once threatened by the imposed need for modernization are now called back into the shaping of daily activities. The division between a Westernized elite, setting up modernizing programmes from the level of the state down, and the bulk of a population holding religious beliefs, pre-national loyalties, family and clan ties is currently being challenged by a new elite encouraging millions of people to actualize old traditions which are now being turned into revolutionary elements. For instance, in the West the return of the veil is usually denounced as a symbol of Muslim women's oppression. However, from an Islamic perspective it has been argued that the veil entails 'the assertion of independence, separate identity and a rejection of Western cultural imperialism'.[17] The veil is presented 'not as an imposed constraint on women's freedom of movement and self-actualization, but as a deliberate act of choice, influenced by the Iranian Revolution, which springs from a certain view of what an Islamic society should be'.[18] The veil stands as a symbol of the wish to restore a traditional morality that is being actualized, a morality that rejects the Western models lying at the heart of the messages spread thanks to globalization. From this perspective, the return of the veil is an example of rejection of a globally expanded idea about what a modern woman should look like.

Islamic Fundamentalism presents an alternative to the culture of modernity propagated by Western political and economic powers. But at the same time it takes advantage of Western technology to reproduce and expand its message. The Islamic world comprises one billion people spread out across the globe. Muslims are the majority in some forty–five countries ranging from Africa to Southeast Asia, and they exist in growing and significant numbers in the United States of America, the former Soviet bloc and Europe.[19]

Globalization has made possible the immediate unified response of Muslims to events affecting their community. The Gulf War, civil war in Bosnia, and the unanimous condemnation of *The Satanic Verses* have mobilized thousands of people living in remote enclaves but connected to each other. These three cases are examples of how globalization can contribute to the strengthening of a sense of solidarity amongst the members of a particular group. Globalization favours the distribution of messages to heterogeneous populations who select and reinterpret them according to their own experiences. Global events are, in this sense, filtered through local experiences.

To illustrate this point, it is possible to distinguish at least two ways in which globalization operated in the Gulf War. On the one hand, the Western media emphasized the character of Saddam Hussein as villain, the illegitimacy of the Iraqi invasion of Kuwait and the need for military intervention. On the other, there was a highly unified Muslim response to the Western interpretation of the conflict. Werbner studies the reaction of the British Pakistani community and highlights their construction of a counter-narrative, a 'resistive reading' which cast Saddam Hussein in the role of hero.[20] In Werbner's view, the response of Pakistani Muslims in Britain resembled, and was part of, a transnational Muslim response throughout the Muslim world. In many cases, it implied bitter rejection of the ideas supplied by the local media and hostility against the opinion held by the majority of the population of the country within which the immigrant Muslim community – in this case Britain – was living and working.

Globalization and modernity mediate the ways in which nationalist discourses are produced and circulated, leaders portrayed and events presented. The persistence and reactivation of nationalism and also the revitalization of some religions show the manifest need of individuals to feel part of a group and find a set of ideas worth fighting for and able to give meaning to their lives. The view of nationalism as a movement against the tide of modernity and a return to tribalism frequently sustained by social scientists, turns a blind eye to the fact that nationalism as a political discourse has accompanied modernity since its early stages. Nationalism operated as a legitimizing ideology in the foundation of the nation-state. It defended cultural diversity in the Romantic era, and in the age of globalism it opposes homogenization by articulating a discourse based upon the value of individual cultures and the rights of peoples to decide their political destiny.

Conclusion

In this book, I have sought to make a contribution to the study of nationalism by concentrating upon two aspects of the phenomenon: the analysis of nationalism in terms of its political, social and psychological elements, and the distinction between 'state nationalism' and the nationalism of 'nations without a state'. In drawing this book to a close I shall offer a summary of the main arguments I have developed and attempt to explore the features of contemporary nationalism when compared with its earlier forms in the late nineteenth and early twentieth centuries.

From the state system that was once one of the peculiarities of Europe, there has developed a system of nation-states covering the globe in a network of national communities. A variety of factors were involved in this: the combination of industrial and military power developed by the European states; the expansion of the administrative power of such states; the influence of a series of contingent historical developments such as the period of relative peace in Europe dating from the treaties of 1815; the acceleration of technological innovation in weaponry; and the formal recognition of the autonomy and 'boundedness' of the nation-state made in the treaties following the First World War. All of this eventually led to the creation of a reflexively monitored system of nation-states at a global level. The point is not so much the acknowledgement of any particular state boundaries, but recognition of the authenticity of the nation-state as the legitimate arbiter of its own 'internal' affairs and as a political actor *par excellence*.[1] However, the fact is that the nation-state is far from being hegemonic; in other words, most Western

European states – as with states elsewhere – are, to a varying degree, multinational.[2]

Nationalism contributed to the rise of the nation-state by providing its myths of origin. It also helped to create links of solidarity that have proved able to block off other possible discursive articulations of interest. The multinational character of the majority of the nation-states has generated a nationalism opposed to that instilled by the state; this is the nationalism of nations without a state. We find two types of nationalism that confront each other and are basically distinguished by the different access to power and resources they possess. Nationalism accorded legitimacy to the nation-state; today, the nationalism of minorities undermines this legitimacy and contributes to the transformation of the nation-state.

Although the accounts of nationalism offered in classical social thought contain significant shortcomings, it is worthwhile pursuing certain lines of enquiry they open up. Treitschke's and Weber's nationalist attitude identifies the political character of nationalism, emphasizing the relation between nationalism, the nation-state and power. Their approach perfectly exemplifies state nationalism and its major trends: the tendency to homogenize the people of the state and the urgency of the demand to construct a powerful nation. These lines of thought have been elaborated in chapter two, where I have developed my own discussion of the political character of nationalism.

Marx's contribution to the study of nationalism is twofold. First, in his view, it refers to the need of a nation to be free from its conquerors as a pre-condition for the assumption of international aims. This argument is closely related to the claims of contemporary minorities' nationalist movements seeking recognition within the states that contain them. Second, Marx calls attention to the relevance of economic factors in the construction of a nationalist discourse. A further dimension, of course (although one not discussed here) is the impact of nationalisms associated with Marxism in movements that have sprung up in many Third World countries in the past.

Durkheim's theory of religion takes on particular poignancy when applied to nationalism. In Durkheim's view, the idea of society is the 'soul of religion'. Nationalism worships society and proves able to generate strength, solidarity and a sense of transcendence similar to those inspired by religion. Here, I have explored the relevance to the theory of nationalism of Durkheim's analysis of symbolism and ritual; but I have also sought to move beyond his assumptions by linking his theories – including his account of the state – in a direct way with nationalism.

At this point I shall try to draw together in a systematic way the main arguments developed in this dissertation. Nationalism, I argue, can only be successfully understood if two major dimensions of it are taken on board: these are its political character and its role in creating identity. The political character of nationalism stems from its quality as a doctrine closely linked to the territoriality of the nation-state. This reconceptualization of legitimacy is a product of the expansion of ideas of popular sovereignty and democracy that emerged following the French and American Revolutions. It fostered a slow and contested process by means of which individuals were recognized as possessing rights to influence the ways in which the future of their communities should develop. Citizenship and its outcome, the right to decide upon one's nation's political destiny, had to be struggled for. In this context, nationalism proved successful in moving people's loyalties away from the monarch and fostering the nation as a new kind of attachment. The political dimension of nationalism brought into a (conflictual) relation the Enlightenment doctrines and the emphasis of the Romantics upon the underlying importance of cultural and linguistic diversity. Nationalism not only reinforced the nation-state building process, at the same time it contained the seeds of new tensions affecting national minorities included within the boundaries of already established nation-states.

Gellner defines nationalism as 'the political principle which holds that the political and the national unit should be congruent'. However, as he points out, only rarely do we find that nation and state are coextensive, and hence there exist many examples of the violation of the nationalist principle. Its most intolerable infringement, from the nationalist point of view, occurs when the rulers of the political unit belong to a nation other than that of the majority of the ruled. Gellner makes this point, arguing that: 'nationalism is a theory of political legitimacy, which requires that ethnic boundaries should not cut across political ones, and, in particular, that ethnic boundaries within a given state should not separate the power-holders from the rest.'[3]

A difficult question constantly recurs when dealing with nationalism: what makes so many peoples willing to die for their nations? Where does the power of nationalism stem from? Why do people bother about the preservation of their land, culture, language, political institutions and ways of life? One could answer that elites have a special interest in perpetuating the nation they belong to. It could perhaps be argued that it is always more attractive to be a minister, a leading intellectual or an artist of a small country than to have to compete within a much larger entity. This could explain why it makes sense for a writer, a politician or a painter to be nationalist in Catalonia, Scotland or Quebec since their possibilities of success within a small community are greater. But this argument is hardly compelling when one seeks to explain why a fisherman, a farmer, a factory worker or a housewife should exhibit nationalist feelings, and stresses the ability of nationalism to bring together people from different social and cultural backgrounds.

The strength of nationalism derives above all from its ability to create a sense of identity. In a world fraught with doubt, fragmentation and lack of ideologies capable of generating meaning in the life of individuals, nationalism becomes a potent force. Hroch argues, 'nationalism is a substitute for factors of integration in a disintegrating society. When society fails, the nation appears as the ultimate guarantee.'[4] Common culture, land, a myth of origin, the will to construct a common future and when at all possible, language, are basic elements that favour the emergence of a common consciousness. Culture facilitates a specific solidarity by means of which individuals relate to themselves, others and nature. But, even more important, culture permits individuals to establish a distinction between 'insiders' and 'outsiders'. The nation is the socio-historical context within which culture is embedded, and by means of which culture is produced, transmitted and received. The emotional investment that individuals make in their land, language, symbols and beliefs generates the drive to self-determination.

Nationalism draws on tradition as an element that transcends the life of individuals. However, nationalism also involves a continuous dynamic process in which symbols are constantly re-created and assigned new meanings, according to the changing circumstances through which the life of the community develops. The performance of common rituals enhances the sentiment of unity among the members of the nation. The display of certain symbols identified with the life of the group arouses deep passionate feelings that cannot be reduced to rational causation. The power of nationalism can only be accounted for if we acknowledge that there is a side of nationalism that belongs to the realm of emotions and irrationality.

Nationalism is Janus-faced. This derives from the two possible ways in which the force of nationalism can be articulated. Nationalism can be associated with authoritarian regimes that place the interest of their nation above everything and aim at economic, cultural and political expansion. In these cases nationalism is employed to justify the superiority of one group above others and 'outsiders' are either killed, expelled or assimilated. The particular solution depends on the political ideology accompanying nationalism. This type of nationalism stands as a phenomenon not reducible to, but primarily found among, state nationalisms. National Socialism in Germany, Fascism in Italy and Francoism in Spain can be given as examples.

The prevalence of nationalism is perceived as a moral scandal by some social scientists 'because the official ethical culture of almost the entire world is a universalist ethical culture'.[5] Such claims give prominence to the nationalisms which attempt to enforce the cultural, economic and political interest of a nation to the direct damage of that of others, but absolutely ignore the rational and moral core of the nationalist demands of minorities who ask the right to exist, be respected and develop their own culture and identity. The neglect of such a distinction fails to notice the power of a kind of nationalism that entails cultural resistance and challenges modern societies by vindicating what I have called 'identity politics', that is, the claim for cultural difference based upon ethnicity. This type of nationalism, I argue, can be regarded as a progressive social movement close to feminist or green movements in so far as it attempts to give a voice to those who had been silenced. The nationalism of minorities such as the Catalans, the Scots or the Kurds raises ethical issues by questioning the legitimacy of certain states as representatives of the people they rule. The preservation of, at least, the cultural existence of the nation is the main objective of this form of nationalism that vindicates rights for all members of the community, particularly the right to be 'different'. In political terms, this type of nationalism demands autonomy to control a living space (which in this case is also a geographic territory) and fights for new channels of representation by claiming access to decision-making processes affecting its community.

The future of nationalism

Future forms of nationalism in Western Europe are likely to exhibit and accentuate a set of characteristics present in contemporary nationalisms and distinct from those of the late nineteenth or early twentieth centuries. These are: first, the appeal to democracy and popular sovereignty as legitimizing agents within the nationalist discourse. Cultural resistance is defended as a means of protecting the heritage of a particular group and presupposes a positive attitude towards diversity. Democracy comes to the fore as a doctrine based upon the acknowledgement that people should be able to speak up and take part in decision-making processes affecting them. Armed struggle, in this context, can no longer be justified when there is a possibility for open dialogue between the state and the national minority involved. The mutual acceptance of democracy and popular sovereignty as guiding principles for political action compels the state and the national minority engaged in the conflict to find a peaceful solution – whether it be a certain autonomy or independence as a new political institution – and abandon the use of violence.

In some cases, if the minorities' representatives are recognized and given the right to negotiate the future of their community, the offer to stop armed struggle forces the state to reconsider an initially hostile attitude towards the aspirations of a national minority that on many occasions is not even named as such. The maintenance of a constant state of alert to prevent the attacks organized by resistance groups requires the mobilization of the army and a high budget to sustain it; it also demands a constant actualization of a political discourse which denies the legitimacy of the minority's claims. Often the situation cannot be sustained over a long period; international opinion, the internal stability of the state, the high economic cost involved in designing and implementing a defence policy, and the eventual success of the national minority in presenting their case to the international community, press for a political solution. However, there do exist cases in which a minority has been denied not only the right to political self-determination, but any chance to maintain and cultivate its culture and language for remarkably long periods of time. Catalans and Basques suffered repression for forty years under Franco, and Palestinians have only recently been granted political recognition in Israel (1994), while a process that might lead to self-determination for the Kurdish people has not yet been initiated.

The current proliferation of struggles for self-determination in several parts of the world indicates that the desire of nation-states to present themselves as democratic does not necessarily result in the adoption of a dialogic attitude towards the national minorities they contain. The use of force remains a key feature in the definition of the nation-state, and its territorial integrity is hardly ever questioned. The delicate equilibrium of the nation-state system relies heavily upon the assumption that each state's sovereignty has to be respected and defended. Non-intervention in 'internal affairs' is a quasi-sacred norm amongst nation-states. But the economic and political power of the nation-state in question and the possible repercussions of an international recognition of the legitimacy of the minority's claims – an expansion of the conflict, an unstoppable and unwanted flow of refugees, or an alteration of so far beneficial political or economic agreements – impact upon the ways in which the international community might respond. Democracy and popular sovereignty may be twisted and given substantially different meanings to suit the interests of the most powerful contender. Hope stems from some supranational bodies' will to intervene and prevent the violation of human rights wherever conflict emerges. But up to the present time the task of international organizations such as the United Nations has mostly been restricted to the open condemnation of atrocities, and only in very few cases have they been able actually to impede or halt them.

Second, the role of nationalism as a mass movement. Nationalism has played a crucial part in the conscription of large armies and the waging of war. Currently nationalism appeals to wide-ranging sectors of the population and stands as a dynamic agent that not only relies on violence, but is able to promote peaceful mass mobilization. The call for independence in some former USSR countries, such as the Baltic Republics, stands as an example of the force acquired by mass movements supporting particular claims.

The second half of the twentieth century can be portrayed as a period in which numerous initially minoritarian movements have emerged and frequently transformed themselves into mass movements with a potential for high socio-political impact. Feminists, greens, pacifists, gays, blacks, animal-rights defenders and national minorities are some of the most prominent groups which have become, at different points in time and in different places, unexpected mass movements. They all require charismatic leaders having the skill to articulate a convincing discourse based upon the urgent need to redress a state of affairs perceived as unjust. They all advocate change and refer to the movement's aims as a crucial component of their identity. These movements awake strong feelings among their followers, who are usually ready to put forward an intense emotional defence of their cause.

The eminently strong potential of nationalism to arouse the masses brings to the fore once more the human inclination towards the performance of rituals able to create or enhance a sense of community, and engender feelings of solidarity towards fellow members of the group. The understanding of nationalism as a political discourse that has its basis in kinship and pre-modern ties makes it suitable as a form of ideology seeking the reconstruction of a sense of community. When individuals feel isolated and ideologies collapse, the appeal to nationalism proves successful in binding people together. It offers them a chance of closeness which stems from the pursuit of a common aim. Nationalism is likely to be invoked in the foreseeable future to resist homogenization, overcome political crisis, divert attention from more crucial matters, oppose the increasing power of international and supranational organizations and give meaning to economic, political and social struggles.

Third, the contemporary erosion of a clear-cut class-divided society contributes to the advent of a form of nationalism that easily spreads across social boundaries. The lack of ideologies able to exercise the appeal once enjoyed by socialism reinforces the power of a nationalist discourse addressed to all those who form a community, ignoring their social backgrounds, proposing to them common goals from which, if attained, they will benefit. The complexity of class structure in the West is likely to be accentuated. Changing patterns in the workplace, increasing interdependence between countries and the internationalization of labour and capital are facilitating the emergence of new professional groups who do not identify with the working class although they have to rely on a salary – most people do rely on a salary anyway – but who fall short of perceiving themselves as the traditional Marxian 'capitalist'.

In my view, the increasingly wide gap between the affluent and those lacking financial or other means of subsistence, the progressive dismantling of the welfare state system, and the relentless rise of the Right in the United States and some European countries, could halt the magnetic power of nationalism unless a common enemy is found or an engaging new project successfully endorsed.

In the near future the nationalism of nations without a state will continue to gain strength. A common aim, the achievement of political recognition, has proved potent enough to blur class differences and relocate individual identity around concepts related to the cultural and political aspects of national identity. Greater instability may be expected in the lands of the former Soviet Union where nationalism will occupy a prominent place in the transitional period that will be needed to spread new ideologies able to take the place of communism. Religion will increase its power and play a key role in the reconstruction of national identities. In many instances we shall witness a reappropriation of religion as a mechanism seeking the actualization of tradition; as a body of values and ideas which can be reinterpreted and employed as a 'book of answers' to day-to-day problems. The current re-emergence of Islamic Fundamentalism can be seen as a response to globalization and a rejection of modernity. It claims to bring back tradition and holds an enormous power as a force capable of addressing the questions faced by contemporary individuals concerning civil and political aspects of societal life.

The reluctance to give away sovereignty and lose control over domestic matters – although economic, political and social problems can no longer be solved internally and show a somewhat unstoppable tendency to reveal the impact of transnational forces and global interdependencies – will increase the presence of nationalism in the nation-state's political discourses. Here we shall see a growth of contradictory forces; the need to participate in international forums and institutions and the search for the establishment of common policies which could contribute to the world's well-being and stability are likely to run into difficulties resulting from the state's desire to protect its own interests. The forthcoming referendum about the adoption of a single European currency, as well as any public consultation on issues that may undermine the state's decision-making power in favour of a supranational organization, will be accompanied by a significant magnification of nationalist arguments for the preservation of the integrity and identity of the nation-state. To be successful, such discourses should attempt to reach a wide range of people across class boundaries, and whatever the message they choose to disseminate – for or against a single currency in this particular case – this will involve putting forward a unified image of the nation-state. Nationality, and arguments around the idea that 'this is best for our country', will be a clear appeal for the strengthening of national identity above all other sources of group membership, including class.

A third form of nationalism that may emerge in the foreseeable future is one embracing citizens of several nation-states to form some kind of supranational organization. The European Union, if it should progress, will surely develop a certain new brand of nationalism that will not erase local identity. Such nationalism will be invoked whenever common action is needed in the economic, social or political arena to fight a common enemy or defend the prosperity of the Union. The wish to stop immigration from poor countries into Europe contains the seeds for eventual solidarity amongst European partners and could ultimately favour the advent of this supranational nationalism. The political discourse of supranational nationalism will ignore class structures and address the ordinary European citizen as if such a category existed above other sources of identity and determined a certain status shared by all individual members. The critical issues here will be how to frame a specifically European identity and which groups will be considered as 'outsiders'.

Fourth, the dramatic technological revolutions of recent years have increased the ways in which symbolic forms in modern societies become mediated by the mechanisms and institutions of mass communication. Nationalism relies heavily upon mass communication as a means of spreading cultural symbols, enhancing the image of leaders who embody popular aspirations, and disseminating new ideas and values. Nationalist discourses, as well as other political messages, are immediately produced and expanded to diffuse, reinterpret or reject all sorts of initiatives affecting the life of the nation. Access to the tremendous power of the media depends on the resources available to each nationalist organization. The uneven use of the media by nationalist groups reflects the various degrees of power they enjoy and has significant repercussions upon the public image they are able to display both to the national community and the international audience.

An intense and widespread use of the media turns leaders into familiar faces who often break into the intimacy of domestic life. Their smiles, words and manners become indistinguishable from the political messages they proclaim when appealing to the individual's inner desire for transcendence, identity and the security and strength emanating from the consciousness of belonging to a group. Undoubtedly the media possess an indefinite number of possible ways in which messages can be spread, and access to them multiplies the chances of success of any political organization. Mass communication will continue to occupy a prominent part in the construction and dissemination of nationalist discourses and this will presumably intensify conflict and rivalry between groups seeking the monopoly of such a powerful alliance.

Fifth, contemporary nationalisms use tradition in the service of modernity. The nation, as Touraine remarks, is a 'non-modern actor that creates modernity', and while seeking to keep it under control, has to accept a weakening of its role in favour of internationalism.[6] The present uncertainty that cuts across all areas of knowledge is strongly connected to the human race's imperfect control of nature and the proliferation of unintended consequences of human action. Doubt and fragmentation are eminent in modernity because they are unexpected. They have existed in other periods, but then they were accepted as a consequence of the difficulty of understanding the functioning of the universe and its creatures. The absence of a single officially sanctioned method of knowledge reflected a certain kind of fragmentation that differs from the one present in our time. The Enlightenment promised rational knowledge if certain methods were observed. Modernity proclaims the failure of reason as a guiding principle, which has certainly opened up numerous possibilities and contributed to impressive scientific and technological advances but has not given mankind absolute control over naturally and humanly produced threats and dangers.

The return to tradition – or, to be more precise, the selective use of tradition and its reinterpretation to fulfil current demands – emphasizes the value of continuity in a context where constant change and adaptation to new social, political and technological environments determine the day-to-day life of individuals. The concept of nation as an entity rooted in pre-modern times, and the perception of culture and language as products of the evolvement of a community over a long period, will retain their strong power to attract individuals. Tradition will continue to be invoked as a legitimizing principle only in so far as it is constantly actualized. The new elements brought about by modernity will inexorably be incorporated into and mixed with traditional forms of life.

Finally, the dialogue between cultures prompted by globalization affects all regions of the world and radically transforms the message of nationalism since isolation and (to some extent) ignorance of the 'other' are no longer possible. Globalization intensifies the individual's consciousness of diversity by showing how different cultures select certain items of an initially neutral world and charge them with meaning. However, globalization is not homogeneous; rather, it implies that while some cultures become widespread and are regarded as a symbol of status – linked to the political and economic power of the nation to which the culture belongs – others are portrayed as showing the curious reluctance of certain groups not to give up an 'outdated' and 'unfit' culture only suited to satisfying the ethnographic curiosity of a few anthropologists.

The uneven access of cultures to the channels that facilitate the dissemination of their messages determines their possibility of achieving a global dimension. Globalization unleashes a pressing demand for identity amongst those individuals who regard the totality of the inherited ideas, beliefs, values, and knowledge that constitute the shared bases of their lives as threatened by the expansion of alien cultures endowed with greater resources. In many cases nationalism emerges as a response to progressive homogenization and represents a struggle to defend 'identity politics'. There are also occasions when nationalism is connected to ideologies that are actively pursuing the enhancement of their own nation and culture whilst undermining those of others. The rejection of the different is central to fascist and racist discourses, and often involves the use of force in preventing the free progress of other groups considered as inferior. The strength and wide diffusion of certain values and ideas activates a mechanism by which local fabulations of global messages radically transform them, thus reversing the homogenizing potential of globalization. In the near future globalization processes are likely to be intensified, but the emergence of a 'global identity' is not yet on the agenda simply because it would be ill-suited to fulfil the needs of an otherwise diverse population.

In considering the future of nationalism it is necessary to add a final remark and account for its role in Third World countries. In these areas, nationalism acted as an imported ideology which proved successful in binding together a heterogeneous population fighting colonialism. Once independence was achieved, nationalism led to the reconstruction of indigenous identities and informed the 'nation-building' processes by which the new elites sought to legitimize the states they inherited from the previous colonial rulers. Future concerns of nationalists in the Third World will include the search for economic independence from the West and the active reappropriation of foreign cultural items received through the media in order to enable the emergence and development of autochthonous national identities.

In the Third World conflict will be unavoidable and will stem primarily from two main sources: the differences arising between the ethnic groups included in the mostly arbitrarily created states received from the colonial period, and the wide gap between a small affluent elite and large numbers of people living in conditions of poverty. In the first case, nationalism is likely to be employed as a weapon to ignite old antagonisms and disputes; in the second, it could either be used to propose alternative images of the nation, or be channelled to blame the West for any troubles that arise. Resentment of Western exploitation might favour the spread of alternative values and life-styles more or less connected to indigenous traditions. A nationalist component will be present in such movements, since the restoration of the nation inevitably includes the protection of its culture.

Notes

Introduction

1 Gellner, *Nations and Nationalism*, pp. 51–2.
2 Deutsch, *Nationalism and Social Communication*, p. 101.
3 Kedourie, *Nationalism*, p. 80.
4 Nairn, *The Break-up of Britain*, pp. 351–3.
5 Smith, A. D. *National Identity*, p. 176.
6 Anderson, B. *Imagined Communities*, pp. 19 and 47.
7 Smith, A. D. 'Nationalism and classical social theory'.

Chapter 1   Nationalism in Classical Social Theory

Abbreviations

The following abbreviations are used for works which are frequently cited in the notes to this chapter:

DL   Durkheim, *The Division of Labour in Society*.
LE   Durkheim, 'L'État'.
LS   Durkheim, *Leçons de Sociologie*.
SP   Durkheim, *Sociology and Philosophy*.
EF   Durkheim, *The Elementary Forms of the Religious Life*.
SU   Durkheim, *Suicide*.
WGP Mommsen, *Max Weber and German Politics (1890–1920)*.
FA   Weber, M. 'The National State and Economic Policy'.
ES   Weber, M. *Economy and Society*.

1 Treitschke, *Selections from Treitschke's lectures on politics*, p. 8.
2 Treitschke, *Politics*, vol. l, p. 30.
3 Ibid. p. 271.
4 Ibid. p. 29.

5 Ibid. p. 19.
6 Treitschke, *Selections*, p. 26.
7 Davis, *The political thought of H. von Treitschke*, p. 150.
8 Ibid. p. 107.
9 Ibid. p. 153.
10 Treitschke, *Selections*, p. 23.
11 Ibid. p. 32.
12 Treitschke, *Politics*, p. 105.
13 Treitschke, *Selections*, p. 39.
14 Davis, *The political thought of H. von Treitschke*, p. 122.
15 Treitschke, *Selections*, p. 67.
16 Ibid. p. 12.
17 Davis, *The political thought of H. von Treitschke*, p. 23.
18 Ibid. p. 106.
19 Treitschke, *Politics*, p. 15.
20 Ibid. p. 15.
21 Davis, *The political thought of H. von Treitschke*, p. 186.
22 Treitschke, *Selections*, p. 11.
23 Davis, *The political thought of H. von Treitschke*, p. 189.
24 Ibid. p. 186.
25 Treitschke, *Selections*, p. 19.
26 Ibid. p. 123.
27 Treitschke, *Politics*, p. 273.
28 Davis, *The political thought of H. von Treitschke*, p. 127.
29 Treitschke, *Politics*, p. 21.
30 Treitschke, *Selections*, p. 10.
31 Treitschke, *Politics*, p. 281.
32 Davis, *The political thought of H. von Treitschke*, p. 16.
33 Marx & Engels, 'Manifesto of the Communist Party' in *Basic Writings on Politics and Philosophy*, p. 49.
34 Bloom, *The World of Nations*, p. 76.
35 Ibid. p. 77, quoted from *Das Kapital*.
36 Marx, 'Contribution to the Critique of Hegel's Philosophy of Right' in Tucker (ed.) *The Marx-Engels Reader*, p. 65.
37 Ibid. p. 65.
38 For a detailed explanation, see Szporluk, *Communism and Nationalism*.
39 Ibid. p. 35.
40 Marx, *The German Ideology*, p. 78.
41 Marx & Engels, *Basic Writings on Politics and Philosophy*, p. 65.
42 Ibid. p. 60.
43 Marx, K. article on F. List's book *Das Nationale System der Politischen Ökonomie*, in Marx & Engels *Collected Works*, vol. 4, p. 280.
44 Marx & Engels, *Collected Works*, vol. 4, p. 298.
45 Marx & Engels, *Basic Writings on Politics and Philosophy*, p. 53.
46 'Account of Engels' speech on Mazzini's attitude towards the International' in Marx & Engels, *Collected Works*, vol. 22, p. 608.
47 Marx & Engels, *Basic Writings on Politics and Philosophy*, p. 61.
48 'Engels' record of his report at the General Council Meeting at May 14, 1872' in Marx & Engels, *Collected Works*, vol. 23, p. 154.
49 Ibid. p. 155.

50 Ibid. p. 156.
51 Marx & Engels, *Basic Writings on Politics and Philosophy*, p. 60.
52 Ibid. pp. 65–6.
53 Marx & Engels 'Critique of the Gotha Programme' in *Basic Writings on Politics and Philosophy*, p. 163.
54 It may be useful to see 'Communist Nationalism' in Smith, A. D. *Nationalism*.
55 LS p. 48 and see also Durkheim, E. 'A debate on nationalism and patriotism' in *Libres entretiens*, series 1, translated in Giddens, *Durkheim on Politics and the State*.
56 LE p. 435 and see also LS p. 50. The author has made all translations from French. Original text: 'L'état est donc avant tout un organe de reflexion . . . c'est l'intelligence mise à la place de l'instinct obscur.'
57 LS p. 54.
58 Ibid. p. 56.
59 LE p. 437 and see also LS p. 57. Original text in LE: 'L'état devient fort, actif, plus l'individu devient libre. C'est l'état qui le libere.'
60 SP p. 55.
61 LS p. 65.
62 SU p. 384.
63 LE p. 437. Original text: 'L'état . . . lui aussi a besoin d'être contenu par l'ensemble des forces secondaires qui lui sont subordonnées sans quoi, comme tout organe que rien n'arrête, il se développe sans mesure et devient tyrannique et se force.'
64 Ibid. p. 435.
65 DL p. 167.
66 LE p. 435.
67 Ibid. p. 435.
68 DL p. liv, and see also LS p. 63.
69 SU p. 389.
70 Durkheim, *Éducation et Sociologie*, p. 60. Original text: 'l'éducation assure entre les citoyens une suffisante communauté d'idées, et de sentiments sans laquelle toute société est impossible.'
71 LE p. 437.
72 Durkheim, E. *L'Allemagne au-dessus de tout*, p. 46.
73 Ibid. p. 45.
74 LS p. 80.
75 Ibid. p. 96.
76 LE p. 437.
77 Giddens remarks on this particular point in his book *Durkheim on Politics and the State*.
78 LS p. 104.
79 EF p. 419.
80 Ibid. p. 206.
81 Ibid. p. 417.
82 Ibid. p. 427.
83 Ibid. p. 230.
84 Gellner, *Reason and Culture*, p. 36.
85 EF p. 419.
86 Gellner, *Nations and Nationalism*, p. 56.

87 Gellner, *Reason and Culture*, p. 37.
88 Ibid. p. 37.
89 Mauss, *Oeuvres*, vol. 3, p. 476.
90 Durkheim, 'A debate on Nationalism and Patriotism' translated by Giddens in *Durkheim on Politics and the State*, p. 206.
91 LS p. 48.
92 Durkheim, 'A debate on Nationalism and Patriotism' translated by Giddens in *Durkheim on Politics and the State*, p. 206.
93 Ibid. p. 206.
94 Durkheim, 'Pacifisme et Patriotisme', p. 103.
95 Giddens, A. *Durkheim on Politics and the State*, p. 202.
96 Ibid. p. 203.
97 Ibid. p. 201.
98 Durkheim, 'Pacifisme et Patriotisme', p. 101.
99 Giddens, *Durkheim on Politics and the State*, p. 201.
100 Durkheim, 'Pacifisme et Patriotisme', p. 101.
101 Durkheim, *L'Allemagne au-dessus de tout*, p. 44. Original text: 'C'est le besoin de s'affirmer, de ne rien sentir au-dessus de soi, l'impatience de tout ce qui est limité et dépendance, en un mot, la volonté de puissance . . . Pour justifier son besoin d'être souveraine, elle s'est naturellement attribué toutes les supériorités; puis, pour rendre intelligible cette supériorité universelle, elle lui a cherché des causes dans la race, dans l'histoire, dans la légende.'
102 Durkheim, *Qui a voulu la guerre?*, p. 61. Original text: 'il n'existe pas à l'actif de l'Allemagne un seul geste sérieux de paix, mais rien que de vaines paroles.'
103 Ibid. p. 63.
104 Ibid. p. 54. Original text: 'en fait, elle a, jusqu'au bout et de toutes ses forces, lutté pour la paix . . . l'attitude extérieure de la France fut toujours d'une irréprochable correction.'
105 Giddens, *Durkheim on Politics and the State*, p. 202.
106 SU p. 390.
107 DL p. liv.
108 Weber, M. 'Politics as a Vocation' in *From Max Weber: Essays in Sociology*, p. 78.
109 Ibid.
110 ES vol. I, p. 395.
111 Ibid. p. 389.
112 Ibid. p. 389.
113 Ibid. p. 390.
114 Ibid. p. 395.
115 Weber, M. *From Max Weber: Essays in Sociology*, p. 178.
116 Ibid. p. 176.
117 WGP p. 238.
118 Weber, M. *From Max Weber: Essays in Sociology*, p. 172.
119 ES p. 398.
120 FA p. 438.
121 WGP p. 53.
122 Beetham, *Max Weber and the theory of Modern Politics*, p. 131.
123 Albrow, M. *Max Weber's Construction of Social Theory*, p. 81.
124 Ibid. p. 82.

125 FA p. 438.
126 Ibid. p. 446.
127 ES p. 926.
128 Ibid. p. 910.
129 Ibid. p. 911. See also p. 926: '(Power) including economic power, may be valued for its own sake. Very frequently the striving for power is also conditioned by the social honor it entails. Not all power, however, entails social honor ... Quite generally, "mere economic" power, and especially "naked" money power, is by no means a recognized basis of social honor. Nor is power the only basis of social honor ... Power, as well as honor, may be guaranteed by the legal order, but, at least normally, it is not their primary source.'
130 FA p. 434.
131 WGP p. 47.
132 Weber, M. *From Max Weber: Essays in Sociology*, p. 121.
133 Ibid. pp. 124–6.
134 FA p. 446.
135 Ibid. p. 432.
136 Ibid. p. 438.
137 Ibid. p. 438.
138 Ibid. p. 434.
139 WGP p. 79.
140 WGP p. 191.
141 For the German war aims from 1914 to 1918 and the flood of memoranda, especially during the first years of the war, see especially Fritz Fischer, *Griff nach der Weltmacht: Die Kriegszielpolitik des Kaiserlichen Deutschlands, 1914–1918*, 3d ed. (Dusseldorf, 1964); Werner Basler, *Deutschlands Annexionspolitik in Polen und im Baltikum 1914–1918*, (Berlin, 1962); Wolfgang Schieder (ed.), *Erster Weltkrieg: Ursachen, Entstehung und Kriegsziele*, Neue Wissenschaftliche Bibliothek, vol. 32 (Cologne, 1969); as well as Mommsen, W. J. on specific aspects partially suggested by Max Weber's critique at the time: 'Die Regierung Bethmann Hollweg und die öffentliche Meinung 1914–1917' *Vierteljahreshefte fur Zeitgeschichte* 17 (1969).
142 WGP p. 321.
143 Ibid. p. 313.
144 Quoted by Mommsen in WGP p. 321.

Chapter 2   The Political Character of Nationalism

1 Giner, S. 'La religión civil', *Diálogo Filosófico* September-December 1991, no. 21 (pp. 357–86) pp. 359–60.
2 Weber, M. *From Max Weber: Essays in Sociology*, p. 78.
3 Another example might be that of Kuwait, whose borders were established in 1913 as a result of a private Turko-British agreement, this being one of many examples of borders redrawn in imperialist map-making. See Jenkins, 'Shifting sands', p. 12.
4 Gellner, *Nations and Nationalism*, p. 1.
5 Giddens, *The Nation-State and Violence*, p. 116.

6 Kohn, *Nationalism*, p. 9.
7 Kedourie, *Nationalism*, p. 58.
8 Herder, *On Social and Political Culture*, p. 324. See also Berlin, *Vico and Herder* and Barnard, *Herder's Social and Political Thought*.
9 See the work of Shils, Geertz, and Fishman on the importance of what Smith calls 'primordial' ties based on language, religion, race, ethnicity and territory.
10 Gellner, *Nations and Nationalism*, p. 55.
11 Gellner, 'Ethnicity, Culture, Class and Power', pp. 237–40.
12 Giddens, *The Nation-State and Violence*, pp. 116–19.
13 Anderson, *Imagined Communities*, p. 14.
14 Armstrong, *Nations before Nationalism*, p. 5.
15 Williams, *When was Wales?*, p. 3.
16 Huizinga, 'Nationalism in the Middle Ages', p. 20.
17 Ibid. p. 17.
18 Smith, A. D. *The Ethnic Origins of Nations*, p. 89.
19 Ibid. pp. 136–7.
20 Heater, *Citizenship*, p. 21.
21 Ibid. p. 23.
22 Kedourie, *Nationalism*, p. 16.
23 Keller, J. A. *The Development of American Citizenship 1608–1870*, p. 341.
24 Giddens, *Sociology*, p. 178.
25 Quoted in Heater, *Citizenship*, p. 70.
26 Ibid. p. 70.
27 Kohn, *Nationalism*, p. 26.
28 Heater, *Citizenship*, p. 57.
29 Nipperdey, 'In Search of Identity', p. 6.
30 Ibid. p. 8.
31 Giddens, *The Nation-State and Violence*, pp. 281–2.
32 Gellner, *Nations and Nationalism*, pp. 37–8.
33 Ibid. p. 38.
34 Giddens, *The Nation-State and Violence*, p. 199.
35 For an illuminating description of Basque nationalism and its development under Franco's dictatorship, see Pérez-Agote, A. *El nacionalismo vasco a la salida del franquismo*.

Chapter 3 National Identity

1 Febvre & Martin, *The Coming of the Book*, p. 323.
2 Ibid. p. 319.
3 Anderson, *Imagined Communities*, pp. 47–8.
4 Graff, *The Legacies of Literacy*, p. 267.
5 Ibid. p. 315.
6 Bowen, *A History of Western Education*, vol. III, p. 467.
7 Graff, *The Legacies of Literacy*, p. 265.
8 Ibid. pp. 286–339.
9 Ibid. p. 276.
10 Ibid. p. 277.
11 Bowen, *A History of Western Education*, p. 463.

12 Gellner, *Nations and Nationalism*, p. 55.
13 See Gellner, 'Nationalism and Politics in Eastern Europe', pp. 127–34.
14 Baumeister, *Identity*, p. 29.
15 Giddens, *Modernity and Self-Identity*, p. 75.
16 Baumeister, *Identity*, p. 59.
17 Yardley & Honess (eds.), *Self-Identity: Psychosocial Perspectives*, p. 121.
18 Baumeister, *Identity*, p. 7.
19 Ibid. p. 18.
20 Ibid. p. 19.
21 Giddens, *Emile Durkheim: Selected Writings*, pp. 222–3.
22 Durkheim, *The Elementary Forms of the Religious Life*, p. 416.
23 Melucci, *Nomads of the Present*, p. 34.
24 Ibid. pp. 89–90.
25 Ibid. p. 91.
26 Ibid. p. 92.
27 Thompson, *Ideology and Modern Culture*, p. 132.
28 Renan, 'What is a nation?', p. 19.
29 Gellner, *Nations and Nationalism*, p. 24. See also by the same author 'The Industrial Division of Labour and National Cultures', p. 273.
30 In personal communication, Professor Ernest Gellner answers my criticism by arguing that in the eighteenth century peasants began to be granted their freedom of movement, came to seek employment in towns, and, therefore, aspired to become managers and clerks. Hence, their linguistic/ cultural identity became important for them. However, to my understanding, in *Nations and Nationalism* he does not make this point explicit.
31 Breuilly, 'Reflections on Nationalism', p. 68.
32 Gellner, *Thought and Change*, p. 147.
33 Gellner, *Nations and Nationalism*, p. 110.
34 During the Francoist regime, the Catalans who sought to defend their dignity by actively protecting their language and culture were systematically excluded from office. To make Gellner's theory plausible, they should have surrendered to the regime's pressure and subscribed to the official culture.
35 Seton-Watson, *Nations and States*, p. xi.
36 Carr, *Nationalism and After*, p. 10.
37 Dunn, 'For the good of the country', p. 1167.
38 Gellner, *Nations and Nationalism*, p. 36.
39 Ibid. p. 110.
40 Dunn, *Western Political Theory in the face of the future*, p. 56.
41 Cohen, *The Symbolic Construction of Community*, p. 12.
42 Ibid. p. 74.
43 Ibid. p. 21.
44 Bertalanffy, *A system view of man*, p. 1.
45 Sperber, *Rethinking Symbolism*, p. 89.
46 Dillistone, *The Power of Symbols*, p. 213.
47 Durkheim, *The Elementary Forms of the Religious Life*, p. 214.
48 Giddens, *Emile Durkheim: Selected Writings*, p. 222.
49 Ibid. p. 223.
50 Ibid. p. 231.
51 Durkheim, *The Elementary Forms of the Religious Life*, p. 230.

Chapter 4 Nationalism, Racism and Fascism

1 Anthias & Yuval-Davis, *Racialized Boundaries*, p. 2.
2 Golberg, *Racist Culture*, p. 81.
3 Ibid. p. 80.
4 See Banton, *The Idea of Race* and Miles, *Racism*.
5 Anthias & Yuval-Davis, *Racialized Boundaries*, p. 4.
6 Cashmore & Troyna, *Introduction to Race Relations*, p. 7.
7 Golberg, *Racist Culture*, p. 150.
8 Spoonley, *Racism & Ethnicity*, p. 4.
9 Anthias & Yuval-Davis, *Racialized Boundaries*, p. 97.
10 Ibid. p. 101.
11 Spoonley, *Racism & Ethnicity*, p. 4.
12 See Gordon & Klug, *New Right, New Racism*.
13 Linz, 'Some notes toward a Comparative Study of Fascism', p. 15.
14 According to Gregor, 'by 1942 the conception of a European consortium of fascist nations united in what was called a "European regime of federal union" had become a commonplace in fascist literature. In 1943 one of the principal planks of the Fascist Republican Party was "the realization of a European community, with a federation of all nations", dedicated to "the abolition of the capitalist system; the struggle against the world plutocracies, and the development, for the benefit of European peoples and of the natives, of Africa's natural resources, with absolute respect for those peoples . . . who . . . have already achieved civil and national organisation".' Gregor, *The Ideology of Fascism*, p. 356.
15 Sternhell, 'Fascist Ideology', p. 335.
16 Dandeker, 'Fascism and ideology', p. 355.
17 Eley, 'Conservatives and radical nationalists in Germany', pp. 52–3.
18 Quoted by Guerin in *Fascism and big business*, p. 68.
19 Quoted by Griffin in *The Nature of Fascism*, p. 8.
20 Mosse, *Masses and Man*, p. 173.
21 Griffin, *The Nature of Fascism*, p. 42.
22 Linz, 'Some notes toward a Comparative Study of Fascism', p. 108.
23 O'Sullivan, *Fascism*, pp. 172–3.
24 Gregor, *The Ideology of Fascism*, p. 173.
25 Ibid. p. 174.
26 O'Sullivan, *Fascism*, p. 175.
27 Mosse, *Masses and Man*, p. 189.
28 Linz, 'Some notes toward a Comparative Study of Fascism', p. 11.
29 Sternhell, 'Fascist Ideology', p. 317.
30 Nolte, *Three Faces of Fascism*, p. 275.
31 Gregor, *The Fascist Persuasion in Radical Politics*, p. 178.
32 Linz, 'Some notes toward a Comparative Study of Fascism', p. 29.
33 Gregor, *The Fascist Persuasion in Radical Politics*, pp. 143–4.
34 Quoted by Brooker in *The Faces of Fraternalism*, pp. 99–100.
35 In January 1933 over 40% of National Socialist Party members were between 21 and 30 years old, 28% between 30 and 40 and only 17% were over 40 years old. Schüddenkopf, *Revolutions of our time: Fascism*, p. 151.
36 See Sternhell, 'Fascist Ideology', p. 341 ff.

37 O'Sullivan, *Fascism*, p. 149.
38 Ibid. see p. 152 ff.
39 Ibid. p. 156.
40 Sternhell, 'Fascist Ideology', p. 328.
41 Ibid. p. 335.
42 Ibid. p. 346.
43 Ibid. p. 345.
44 See Schmitt, *The Concept of the Political* and *Political Theology*.
45 Linz, 'Some notes toward a Comparative Study of Fascism', p. 35.

Chapter 5   Nations without a State

1 Held, D. 'Democracy, the Nation-state and the Global System' in Held, D. (ed.) *Political Theory Today*, p. 200.
2 Brown, *Ethnic Conflict and International Security*, pp. 17–18.
3 Gagnon, 'The Political Uses of Federalism', p. 17.
4 King, *Federalism and Federation*, p. 108.
5 Witte, 'Belgian Federalism', p. 115.
6 See Welsh, 'Domestic Politics and Ethnic Conflict', pp. 50–2.
7 Buchanan, *Secession*, p. 75.
8 Ibid. pp. 29–74.
9 Cooper & Berdal, 'Outside Intervention in Ethnic Conflicts', pp. 188–9.
10 Smith, G. 'The Resurgence of Nationalism' in Smith, G. (ed.) *The Baltic States*, p. 128.
11 Ibid. p. 136.
12 Morris, 'Future Rear' in Bird et al., *Mapping the Futures*, p. 43.
13 Giner, 'The rise of a European Society', p. 147.
14 Aron, 'Old Nations, New Europe', pp. 47–8; Galtung, *Europe in the Making*.
15 Giner, 'The rise of a European Society', p. 149.
16 Baker & Kolinsky, 'The State and Integration', p. 120.
17 Gellner, E. in *Europes: Els intellectuals i la qüestió europea* (Acta, Debat: Barcelona, 1993), p. 259.
18 Giner, 'The rise of a European Society', p. 151.
19 Martin, *Europe: an ever closer union*, p. 18.
20 Aron, 'Old Nations, New Europe', p. 61.

Chapter 6   States without a Nation

1 Akintoye, *Emergent African States*, p. 3.
2 Smith, A. D. *State and Nation in the Third World*, p. 125.
3 Mayall, *Nationalism and International Society*, p. 113.
4 Ibid. p. 117.
5 Ibid. p. 122.
6 Quoted by Bayart in *The State in Africa*, p. 8.
7 Ibid. p. 8.
8 Smith, A. D. *State and Nation in the Third World*, pp. 40–2.
9 Ibid. p. 43.
10 Akintoye, *Emergent African States*, p. 34.

11 Sithole, *African Nationalism*, p. 63.
12 Neuberger, *National Self-Determination in Post-Colonial Africa*, p. 5.
13 See Smith, A. D. *State and Nation in the Third World*, p. 46.
14 Ibid. p. 47.
15 Quoted by Harris in *National Liberation*, p. 168.
16 See chapter 3 in Anderson, *Imagined Communities*.
17 Akintoye, *Emergent African States*, p. 26.
18 Smith, A. D. *State and Nation in the Third World*, pp. 49–50.
19 Neuberger, *National Self-Determination in Post-Colonial Africa*, pp. 9–10.
20 Smith, A. D. *State and Nation in the Third World*, p. 70.
21 Neuberger, *National Self-Determination in Post-Colonial Africa*, p. 17.
22 Sithole, N. *African Nationalism*, p. 2.
23 Smith, A. D. *State and Nation in the Third World*, p. 54.
24 Eisenstadt, quoted by Smith, A. D. *State and Nation in the Third World*, p. 4.
25 See Geertz, *The Interpretation of Cultures*, p. 235.
26 Bayart applies to Africa the distinctions between what he calls 'integral' and 'soft' states. See *The State in Africa*.
27 Geertz, *The Interpretation of Cultures*, p. 239.
28 Ibid. p. 240.
29 Ibid. p. 269.
30 Markakis, *National and Class Conflict in the Horn of Africa*, p. 72.
31 Ibid. p. 73.
32 18% Hindus, 8% Christians, fewer Muslims, 12.5% Sri Lankan Tamils, 6% Indian Tamils and 7.5% Muslims. See Harris, *National Liberation*, p. 209.
33 Ibid. p. 213.
34 Neuberger, *National Self-Determination in Post-Colonial Africa*, p. 50.
35 Bayart, *The State in Africa*, p. 51.
36 Ibid. p. 52.
37 Harris, *National Liberation*, pp. 169–70.
38 Ibid. p. 172.
39 See Tibi, 'The Simultaneity of the Unsimultaneous', p. 146.
40 Ibid. p. 149.

Chapter 7 Globalization, Modernity and National Identity

1 Giddens, *The Consequences of Modernity*, p. 64.
2 Wallerstein, *The Modern World System*. See also by the same author *The Capitalist World Economy*.
3 Appadurai, 'Disjuncture and Difference in the Global Cultural Economy' in Featherstone, *Global Culture: Nationalism, Globalization and Modernity*, pp. 295–310.
4 Tenbruck, F. H. 'The Dream of Secular Ecumene: the meaning and limits of policies of development' in Featherstone, *Global Culture: Nationalism, Globalization and Modernity*.
5 See Ignatieff, M. *Nationalism and the Narcissism of Minor Differences*.
6 Melucci, *Nomads of the Present*, p. 89.
7 Weber, M. *Methodological Essays*, p. 52.
8 Giddens, *The Consequences of Modernity*, p. 105.

9 Laing, *The Divided Self*, p. 43.
10 Ibid. p. 45.
11 Ibid. p. 46.
12 Gellner, *Postmodernism, Reason and Religion*, p. 3.
13 Ibid. p. 2.
14 Esposito, *The Islamic Threat: myth or reality?*, p. 16.
15 Halliday, 'The politics of Islamic fundamentalism', p. 106.
16 Gellner, *Postmodernism, Reason and Religion*, p. 21.
17 Watson, 'Women and the veil', p. 151.
18 Ibid. p. 152.
19 Esposito, *The Islamic Threat: myth or reality?*, p. 4.
20 Werbner, 'Diaspora and millennium', p. 213.

Conclusion

1 Giddens, *The Nation-State and Violence*, p. 255 ff.
2 Llobera, 'Catalan National Identity: dialectics of past and present', p. 248.
3 Gellner, *Nations and Nationalism*, p. 1.
4 Quoted by Hobsbawm in *Nations and Nationalism since 1780*, p. 173.
5 Dunn, J. *Western Political Theory in the face of the future*, pp. 61–2.
6 Touraine, A. *Critique de la Modernité*, p. 162.

Bibliography

Ahmed, A. & Donnan, H. *Islam, Globalization and Postmodernity* (Routledge: London, 1994).

Akintoye, S. A. *Emergent African States* (Longman: London, 1976).

Albrow, M. *Max Weber's Construction of Social Theory* (Macmillan: London, 1990).

Anderson, B. *Imagined Communities: reflections on the origin and spread of nationalism* (Verso: London, 1990 (1983)).

Anthias, F. & Yuval-Davis, N. *Racialized Boundaries: Race, nation, gender, colour and class and the anti-racist struggle* (Routledge: London, 1993).

Appadurai, A. 'Disjuncture and Difference in the global cultural Economy' in Featherstone, M. *Global culture: Nationalism, Globalization and Modernity* (Sage: London, 1990).

Armstrong, J. A. *Nations before Nationalism* (The University of North Carolina Press: Chapel Hill, 1982).

Aron, R. 'Old Nations, New Europe' in Graubard, S. R. *A New Europe?* (Oldbourne Press: London, 1963).

Baker, J. & Kolinsky, M. 'The State and Integration' in Navari, C. *The Condition of States: A Study in International Political Theory* (Open University Press: Milton Keynes, 1991).

Banton, M. *The Idea of Race* (Tavistock: London, 1977).

Barnard, F. M. *Herder's Social and Political Thought: from Enlightenment to Nationalism* (Oxford University Press: Oxford, 1965).

Baumeister, R. *Identity: Cultural Change and the Struggle for Self* (Oxford University Press: Oxford, 1986).

Bayart, J. F. *The State in Africa: The Politics of the Belly* (Longman: London, 1993).

Beetham, D. *Max Weber and the Theory of Modern Politics* (Cambridge: Polity Press, 1985).

Benet, J. *Catalunya sota el regim franquista* (Edicions Catalanes de París: París, 1973).

Bertalanffy, L. von *A systems view of man*, La Violette, P. A. (ed.) (Westview Press: Boulder, Co., 1981).

Berlin, I. *Vico and Herder* (London, 1976).

Bird, J. et al. *Mapping the Futures* (Routledge: London, 1993).

Bisson, T. N. *The Medieval Crown of Aragon* (Clarendon Press: Oxford, 1986).

Bloom, S. F. *The World of Nations: a study of the national implications in the work of Karl Marx* (Columbia University Press: New York, 1941).

Bowen, J. *A History of Western Education* vol. III (Methuen: London, 1981).

Breuilly, J. 'Reflections on Nationalism', *Philosophy of the Social Sciences* no 15, 1985.

Brooker, P. *The Faces of Fraternalism* (Clarendon Press: Oxford, 1991).

Brown, M. (ed.) *Ethnic Conflict and International Security* (Princeton University Press: Princeton, 1993).

Buchanan, A. *Secession: The Morality of Political Divorce from Fort Sunter to Lithuania and Quebec* (Westview Press: Boulder, Colorado, 1991).

Burgess, M. & Gagnon, A. G. *Comparative Federalism and Federation* (Harvester Wheatsheaf: London, 1993).

Carr, E. H. *Nationalism and After* (Macmillan: New York, 1945).

Cashmore, E. E. & Troyna, B. *Introduction to Race Relations* (Routledge & Kegan Paul: London, 1983).

Cheles, L., Ferguson, R. & Vaughan, M. *Neo-Fascism in Europe* (Longman: London, 1991).

Coakley, J. (ed.) *The Social Origins of Nationalist Movements: the Contemporary West European Experience* (Sage Publications: London, 1992).

Cohen, A. P. *The Symbolic Construction of Community* (Tavistock Publications: London, 1985).

Cooper, R. & Berdal, M. 'Outside Intervention in Ethnic Conflicts' in Brown, M. (ed.) *Ethnic Conflict and International Security* (Princeton University Press: Princeton, 1993).

Dandeker, C. *Surveillance, Power & Modernity* (Polity Press: Cambridge, 1990).

Dandeker, C. 'Fascism and Ideology: continuities and discontinuities in capitalist development' in *Ethnic and Racial Studies* vol. 8 number 3, July 1985.

Davis, H. W. C. *The political thought of H. von Treitschke* (Constable & Company: 1914).

Deutsch, K. W. *Nationalism and Social Communication* (The MIT Press: Massachusetts, 1966 (1953)).

Dillistone, F. W. *The Power of Symbols* (SCM Press: London, 1986).

Dunn, J. 'For the good of the country', *Times Literary Supplement*, 21 October 1983.

Dunn, J. *Western Political Theory in the face of the future* (Cambridge University Press: Cambridge, 1979).

Durkheim, E. *L'Allemagne au-dessus de tout: la mentalité allemande et la guerre*, Études et documents sur la guerre (Librairie Armand Colin: Paris, 1915).

Durkheim, E. *Qui a voulu la guerre?: les origines de la guerre d'après les documents diplomatiques* (Librairie Armand Colin: Paris, 1915).

Durkheim, E. *The Elementary Forms of the Religious Life* (George Allen: London, 1982 (1915)).

Durkheim, E. *Education et Sociologie* (Librairie Felix Alcan: Paris, 1922).

Durkheim, E. *Leçons de Sociologie: physique des moeurs et du droit* (Paris, 1950).

Durkheim, E. *Suicide* (Routledge & Kegan Paul: London, 1987 (1952)).

Durkheim, E. 'L'État' in *Revue Philosophique* 83ème année tome CXLVIII (Presses Universitaires de France: Paris, 1958).

Durkheim, E. *Selected Writings* translated by A. Giddens (Cambridge University Press: Cambridge, 1972).

Durkheim, E. 'Pacifisme et Patriotisme' translated by N. Layne in *Sociological Inquiry* 43 (2), pp. 99–103, 1973.

Durkheim, E. *Sociology and Philosophy* (The Free Press: New York, 1974).

Durkheim, E. *The Division of Labour in Society* (Macmillan: London, 1988 (1984)).

Eley, G. 'Conservatives and radical nationalists in Germany: the production of fascist potentials 1912–1928' in Blinkhorn, M. *Fascists and Conservatives* (Unwin Hyman: London, 1990).

Esposito, J. L. *The Islamic Threat: myth or reality?* (Oxford University Press: Oxford, 1992).

Europes: Els intelectuals i la qüestió europea (Acta, Debat: Barcelona, 1993).

Featherstone, M. *Global culture: Nationalism, Globalization and Modernity* (Sage: London, 1990).

Febvre, L. & Martin, H. J. *The Coming of the Book*, Nowell-Smith, G. & Wootton D. (eds) (N.L.B.: London, 1976 (1958)).

Gagnon, A. G. 'The Political Uses of Federalism' in Burguess, M. & Gagnon, A. G. *Comparative Federalism and Federation* (Harvester Wheatsheaf: London, 1993).

Galtung, J. *Europe in the Making* (Crane Russak: New York, 1989).

Geertz, C. *The Interpretation of Cultures* (Fontana Press: London, 1993 (1973)).

Gellner, E. *Thought and Change* (University of Chicago Press: Chicago, 1978 (1965)).

Gellner, E. 'Ethnicity, Culture, Class and Power' in P. F. Sugar, *Ethnic Diversity and Conflict in Eastern Europe* (ABC-Clio: Santa Barbara–Oxford, 1980).

Gellner, E. 'The Industrial Division of Labour and National Cultures', *Government and Opposition* no. 17, 1982.

Gellner, E. *Nations and Nationalism* (Basil Blackwell: Oxford, 1983).

Gellner, E. 'Nationalism and Politics in Eastern Europe', *New Left Review* no. 189, 1991.

Gellner, E. *Reason and Culture* (Blackwell: Oxford, 1992).

Gellner, E. *Postmodernism, Reason and Religion* (Routledge: London, 1992).

Gellner, E. *Encounters with Nationalism* (Blackwell: Oxford, 1994).

Giddens, A. (trans.) *Emile Durkheim: Selected Writings* (Cambridge University Press: Cambridge, 1987 (1972)).

Giddens, A. *Durkheim on Politics and the State* (Fontana Paperbacks: London, 1987 (1978)).

Giddens, A. *The Nation-State and Violence* (Polity Press: Cambridge, 1985).

Giddens, A. *The Consequences of Modernity* (Polity Press: Cambridge, 1990).

Giddens, A. *Modernity and Self-Identity* (Polity Press: Cambridge, 1991).

Giner, S. *Mass Society* (Martin Roberston: London, 1976).

Giner, S. & Archer, M. (eds) *Contemporary Europe: Social Structures and Cultural Patterns* (Routledge & Kegan Paul: London, 1978).

Giner, S. 'The rise of a European Society', *Revue Européenne des sciences sociales*, tome XXXI, 1993 no. 95, pp. 147–61.

Golberg, D. T. *Racist Culture: Philosophy and the Politics of Meaning* (Blackwell: Oxford, 1993).

Gordon, P. & Klug, E. *New Right, New Racism* (Searchlight Publications: London, 1986).

Graff, H. J. *The Legacies of Literacy* (Indiana University Press: Bloomington-Indiana, 1987).

Gregor, A. J. *The Ideology of Fascism* (The Free Press: New York, 1969).

Gregor, A. J. *The Fascist Persuasion in Radical Politics* (Princeton University Press: Princeton, 1974).

Griffin, R. *The Nature of Fascism* (Routledge: London, 1993 (1991)).

Guerin, D. *Fascism and big business* (Monad Press: New York, 1983 (1939)).

Guibernau, M. *El pensament sociológic de Raymond Aron* (Raima Press: Moià, Barcelona, 1988).

Guibernau, M. 'El nacionalismo: ideología de la modernidad?' in *Debats*, number 49, September 1994, pp. 34–9.

Gurruchaga, A. *El código nacionalista vasco durante el franquismo* (Anthtropos: Barcelona, 1985).

Haller, M. 'The Challenge for Comparative Sociology in the Transformation of Europe', *International Sociology* vol. 5 no. 2, June 1990, pp. 183–204.

Halliday, F. 'The politics of Islamic Fundamentalism: Iran, Tunisia and the challenge to the secular state' in Ahmed, A. and Donnan, H. *Islam, Globalization and Postmodernity* (Routledge: London, 1994).

Hamm, B. 'Comparative versus Evolutionary Approaches to European Society' *International Sociology* vol. 6 no. 1, March 1991, pp. 111–17.

Harris, N. *National Liberation* (Penguin Books: London, 1992 (1990)).

Heater, D. *Citizenship: the civil ideal in world history, politics and education* (Longman: London, New York, 1990).

Heiberg, M. 'Inside the moral community: politics in a Basque village' in Douglass, W. A. (ed.) *Basque Politics: A Case Study in Ethnic Nationalism* (Associated Faculty Press and Basque Studies Programme: Reno, NV, 1985), pp. 285–307.

Heiberg, M. *The Making of the Basque Nation* (Cambridge University Press: Cambridge, 1989).

Held, D. (ed.) *Political Theory Today* (Polity Press: Cambridge, 1991).

Herder, J. G. *On Social and Political Culture* translated and edited by F. M. Barnard (Cambridge University Press: Cambridge, 1969).

Hobsbawm, E. J. *Nations and Nationalism since 1780* (Cambridge University Press: Cambridge, 1992 (1990)).

Hroch, M. *Social Preconditions of National Revival in Europe: A Comparative Analysis of the Social Composition of Patriotic Groups among the Smaller European Nations* (Cambridge University Press: Cambridge, 1985).

Huizinga, J. 'Nationalism in the Middle Ages' in Tipton, C. (ed.) *Nationalism in the Middle Ages* (Holt, Rinehart and Winston: New York, 1972).

Hutchinson, J. *Modern Nationalism* (Fontana Press: London, 1994).

Hutchinson, J. & Smith, A. D. (eds.) *Nationalism* (Oxford University Press: Oxford, 1994).

Hylland Eriksen, T. *Ethnicity and Nationalism: Anthropological Perspectives* (Pluto Press: London, 1993).

Ignatieff, M. *Blood and Belonging: Journeys into the New Nationalism* (Chatto & Windus, BBC Books: London, 1993).

Ignatieff, M. *Nationalism and the Narcissism of Minor Differences* (paper published by PAVIS, Centre for Sociological and Social Anthropological Studies: The Open University, 1994).

Jenkins, J. 'Shifting sands', *New Statesman and Society*, 8 February, 1991.

Johnston, H. *Tales of Nationalism: Catalonia (1939–1979)* (Rutgers University Press: New Jersey, 1991).

Joly, D. *The French Communist Party and the Algerian War* (Macmillan: London, 1991).

Kedourie, E. *Nationalism* (Hutchinson University Library: London, 1986 (1960)).

Kellas, J. G. *The Politics of Nationalism and Ethnicity* (Macmillan: London, 1991).

Keller, J. A. *The Development of American Citizenship (1608–1870)* (University of North Carolina Press, 1978).

Khoury, P. S. & Kostiner, J. *Tribes and State Formation in the Middle East* (University of California Press: Oxford, 1990).

King, P. *Federalism and Federation* (Croom Helm: London, 1982).

Kohn, H. *Nationalism: its Meanings and History* (Hutchinson University Library: Princeton, New Jersey, 1965 (1955)).

Laing, R. D. *The Divided Self: an existential study in sanity and madness* (Tavistock Publications: London, 1969 (1960)).

Laqueur, W. (ed.) *Fascism: a reader's guide* (Scolar Press: Cambridge, 1991 (1976)).

Laue, T. H. von *The Global City* (Lippincott Company, J.B.: New York, 1969).

Linz, J. 'Some notes toward a Comparative Study of Fascism in Sociological Historical Perspective' in Laqueur, W. (ed.) *Fascism: a reader's guide* (Scolar Press: Cambridge, 1991 (1976)).

Lorés, J. *La transició a Catalunya (1977–1984): el pujolisme i els altres* (Editorial Empúries: Barcelona, 1985).

Llobera, J. 'Catalan National Identity: the dialectics of past and present' in Tokin, E. et al. *History and Ethnicity* (Routledge: London, 1989).

Llobera, J. 'Catalan Identity', *Critique of Anthropology* vol. 10 nos 2 & 3, winter 1990.

Llobera, J. 'Els canvis a Europa i la crisi dels models clàssics: el futur de les etnonacions dins d'una Europa unida', *Sisenes Jornades. El nacionalisme Català a la fi del segle XX, Reus 1992* (Edicions de la Revista de Catalunya: Barcelona, 1993).

Llobera, J. 'The role of the state and the nation in Europe' in García, S. (ed.) *Europe's Identity and the Search for a New Legitimacy* (Pinter: London, 1993).

Llobera, J. *The God of Modernity* (Berg: London, 1994).

Markakis, J. *National and Class Conflict in the Horn of Africa* (Cambridge University Press: Cambridge, 1987).

Martin, D. *Europe: an ever closer union* (Spokesman for European Labour Forum: Nottingham, 1991).

Marx, K. & Engels, F. *Collected Works* (Lawrence & Wishart: London, 1975).

Marx, K. & Engels, F. *Basic Writings on Politics and Philosophy*, Feuer, L. S. (ed.) (Collins. The Fontana Library: Glasgow, 1976 (1959)).

Marx, K. *The German Ideology*, Arthur, C. J. (ed.) (New York International Publishers: New York, 1978).

Marx, K. 'Contribution to the Critique of Hegel's Philosophy of Right' in Tucker, R. C. (ed.) *The Marx-Engels Reader* (Norton: New York, 1978).

Mauss, M. *Oeuvres*, three volumes (Les éditions du minuit: Paris, 1969).

Mayall, J. *Nationalism and International Society* (Cambridge University Press: Cambridge, 1990).

McCrone, D. *Understanding Scotland: the Sociology of a Stateless Nation* (Routledge: London, 1992).

Melucci, A. *Nomads of the Present* (Hutchinson Radius: London, 1989).

Miles, R. *Racism* (Routledge: London, 1989).

Millennium Journal of International Studies, Winter 1991, vol. 20, number 3. Special issue: 'Reimagining the Nation'.

Molinero, C. & Ysás, P. *L'oposició antifeixista a Catalunya (1939–1950)* (La Magrana: Barcelona, 1981).

Mommsen, W. J. *Max Weber and German Politics (1890–1920)* (The University of Chicago Press: Chicago, 1984).

Mosse, G. L. *Masses and Man* (Howard Fertig: New York, 1980).

Neuberger, B. *National Self-Determination in Post-Colonial Africa* (Lynne Tienner Publishers: Boulder, Colorado, 1986).

Nipperdey, T. 'In Search of Identity' in Eade, J. C. *Romantic Nationalism in Europe* (Humanities Research Centre, Australian National University, 1983).

Nairn, T. *The Break-up of Britain* (New Left Books: London, 1977).

Nolte, E. *Three Faces of Fascism* (Weidenfeld and Nicolson: London, 1965).

O'Sullivan, N. *Fascism* (J. M. Dent & Sons Ltd.: London, 1983).

Pérez-Agote, A. *El nacionalismo vasco a la salida del franquismo* (C.I.S. Ediciones Siglo XXI: Madrid, 1987).

Renan, E. 'What is a nation?' in Bhabha, H. K. (ed.) *Nation and Narration* (Routledge: London, 1990).

Rex, J. *Race and Ethnicity* (Open University Press: Milton Keynes, 1986).

Rokkan, S. & Urwin, D. (eds) *The Politics of Territorial Identity: Studies in European Regionalism* (Sage: London, 1982).

Rokkan, S. & Urwin, D. *Economy, Territory, Identity: Politics of West European Peripheries* (Sage: London, 1983).

Schmitt, C. *The Concept of the Political* (Rutgers University Press: New Brunswick, 1976).

Schmitt, C. *Political Theology: Four chapters on the concept of Sovereignty* (MITT Press: London, 1985).

Schüddenkopf, O. E. *Revolutions of our time: Fascism* (Praeger Publishers: New York, 1973).

Seton-Watson, H. *Nations and States: An enquiry into the Origins of Nations and the Politics of Nationalism* (West View: Boulder, Co. 1977).

Sithole, N. *African Nationalism* (Oxford University Press: London, 1968 (1959)).

Smith, A. D. *Nationalism* (Martin Roberston: Oxford, 1979).

Smith, A. D. 'Nationalism and classical social theory', *The British Journal of Sociology* vol. XXXIV no. 1 March 1983 pp. 19–38.

Smith, A. D. *State and Nation in the Third World* (Wheatsheaf Books: London, 1983).

Smith, A. D. *The Ethnic Origins of Nations* (Basil Blackwell: Oxford, 1986).

Smith, A. D. *National Identity* (Penguin Books: London, 1991).

Smith, G. (ed.) *The Baltic States: the national self-determination of Estonia, Latvia and Lithuania* (Macmillan: London, 1994).

Sperber, D. *Rethinking Symbolism* (Cambridge University Press: Cambridge, 1988 (1975)).

Spoonley, P. *Racism and Ethnicity* (Oxford University Press: Auckland, 1993 (1988)).

Sternhell, Z. 'Fascist Ideology' in Laqueur, W. (ed.) *Fascism: a reader's guide* (Scolar Press: Cambridge, 1991 (1976)).

Szporluk, R. *Communism and Nationalism* (Oxford University Press: Oxford, 1988).

Tejerina, B. 'La dimensión sociocultural del nacionalismo. Continuidad y cambio en la definición de identidad en el nacionalismo vasco', paper presented at the II Congreso Vasco de Sociología, Vitoria 9, 10, 11 April 1992.

Tejerina, B. *Nacionalismo y lengua* (Centro de Investigaciones Sociológicas: Madrid, 1992).

Thompson, J. B. *Ideology and Modern Culture* (Polity Press: Cambridge, 1990).

Tibi, B. 'The Simultaneity of the Unsimultaneous: Old Tribes and Imposed Nation-States in the Modern Middle East' in Khoury, P. S. & Kostiner, J. *Tribes and State Formation in the Middle East* (University of California Press: Oxford, 1990).

Tipton, C. L. (ed.) *Nationalism in the Middle Ages* (Holt, Rinehart and Winston: New York, 1972).

Touraine, A. *Critique de la modernité* (Fayard: Paris, 1992).

Treitschke, H. von *Selections from Treitschke's lectures on politics* (Gowans & Gray: London, 1914).

Treitschke, H. von *Politics* (Constable & Company: London, 1916).

Tucker, R. C. (ed.) *The Marx-Engels Reader* (Norton: New York, 1978).

Vilar, P. *La Catalogne dans l'Espagne moderne* (Flammarion: Paris, 1977).

Vilar, P. (ed.) *Història de Catalunya* (Edicions 62: Barcelona, 1987).

Wallerstein, I. *The Modern World System* (Academic: New York, 1974).

Wallerstein, I. *The Capitalist World Economy* (Cambridge University Press: Cambridge, 1979).

Watson, H. 'Women and the veil: Personal responses to global process' in Ahmed, A. & Donnan, H. *Islam, Globalization and Postmodernity* (Routledge: London, 1994).

Weber, E. *Peasants into Frenchmen: the Modernisation of Rural France, 1870–1914* (Chatto & Windus: London, 1979).

Weber, M. *From Max Weber: Essays in Sociology*, Gerth, H. & Wright Mills (eds) (Routledge: London, 1948).

Weber, M. *Methodological Essays* (The Free Press: New York, 1969 (1949)).

Weber, M. *Economy and Society* (Roth, G. & Wittich, C. (eds) University of California Press: Los Angeles, Berkeley, London, 1978 (1968)).

Weber, M. *Max Weber: Selections in Translation*, Runciman, W. G. (ed.) (Cambridge University Press: Cambridge, 1978).

Weber, M. 'The National State and Economic Policy' (Freiburg Address) in *Economy and Society* vol. 9/4, 1980, pp. 428–49.

Welsh, D. 'Domestic Politics and Ethnic Conflict' in Brown, M. (ed.) *Ethnic Conflict and International Security* (Princeton University Press: Princeton, 1993).

Werbner, P. 'Diaspora and millennium: British Pakistani global-local fabulations of the Gulf War' in Ahmed, A. & Donnan, H. *Islam, Globalization and Postmodernity* (Routledge: London, 1994).

Williams, G. A. *When was Wales?* (Penguin Books: London, 1985).

Witte, E. 'Belgian Federalism: towards Complexity and Asymmetry' in *West European Politics* vol. 15, October 1992, no. 4.

Yardley, K. & Honess, T. (eds) *Self-Identity: Psychosocial Perspectives* (John Wiley & Sons: New York, 1987).

Index